MURDER & CRIME

COUNTY DURHAM

MURDER & CRIME

COUNTY DURHAM

Paul Heslop

The
History
Press

To my children and grandchildren.

First published 2013

The History Press
The Mill, Brimscombe Port
Stroud, Gloucestershire, GL5 2QG
www.thehistorypress.co.uk

© Paul Heslop, 2013

The right of Paul Heslop to be identified as the Author
of this work has been asserted in accordance with the
Copyright, Designs and Patents Act 1988.

British Library Cataloguing in Publication Data.
A catalogue record for this book is available from the British Library.

ISBN 978 0 7524 6751 1

Typesetting and origination by The History Press
Printed in Great Britain

CONTENTS

Foreword

For his most recent work, author and ex-'polis' Paul Heslop has returned to his professional and personal roots to provide us with a fascinating glimpse of crimes past.

In an age where moral panics can be whipped up almost instantly by both social and traditional media, it is tempting to imagine ourselves in a simpler, quieter time – an age where everyone obeyed the rules, a policeman's word was the law and crimes were rare. As Paul reminds us, this mythical 'golden age' never existed. Throughout the last 200 years there are countless examples of serious crime and homicide every bit as shocking to local people then as similar incidents are today.

Using his experience as a major crime investigator, Paul establishes the circumstances surrounding the various cases. Some, like the infamous but barely believable story of serial poisoner Mary Ann Cotton, were the result of careful planning and cool deliberation. Others, like the senseless killing of the unfortunate Acting Sergeant William Smith, appear to have been random acts of violence, often fuelled by drink. Paul also highlights the changes between society's attitudes then and now, and the difference in the criminal justice system.

Much of the 'evidence' submitted in the cases in this book would never had made it to court in the twenty-first century, which may lead us to ponder how many trials were 'fair' to the suspects. But society is constantly evolving, and it is ultimately futile to judge the processes of the past against those of the present.

Paul has written a fascinating and well-researched account of some of County Durham's most notorious crimes. The reader cannot fail to be intrigued by his account, which helps shed light on those dark deeds of long ago.

Mike Barton
Chief Constable, Durham Constabulary, 2013

Foreword

You are about to embark on a journey along the criminal highways and byways of County Durham, stretching from the Victorian days of Empire to the present.

Ex-Detective Inspector Paul Heslop is more than qualified to be your guide. Thirty years in the police force have provided him with an in-depth understanding of crime and criminals. He unpicks the most complex cases, so that we can understand the issues with crystal clarity.

An extra dimension is added by Paul's passionate interest in history. He has lectured widely on topics from Hadrian's Wall and the trials of Bonnie Prince Charlie, to the development of the British Monarchy; he has walked the length and breadth of Britain, researching its local history and publishing his findings in books such as *The Walking Detective* and *One Man's County*, – a 'Johnson and Boswell' journey around Northumberland, his native county. This fascination with history has enabled him to put the crimes he describes into their historical context, vividly bringing to life the periods in which they occur.

What continually surprises in this book is the varied yet repetitious nature of crime, including femme fatale poisons, the late nineteenth-century 'more bobbys on the beat' debate, and a 1930s twist on the battle over immigration and jobs. Finally, at the end of each case, Paul provides comment and assessment, illuminating the criminal landscape through which he has so expertly led us.

Nick Cook, 2013

Nick Cook is a freelance journalist, specialising in health and safety and environmental issues. He teaches creative writing in Hertfordshire and is President of the Verulam Writers Circle, St Albans.

Acknowledgements

I would like to thank staff at County Archives, Durham, and South Tyneside libraries and Information Service for their assistance in the research required to produce this book. Also the staff at the Local Studies sections at Sunderland, Darlington, Hartlepool and Newcastle upon Tyne libraries.

Thanks also to Kathy Douglas and staff at St Peter's Church, Monkwearmouth, for their assistance in my research in Case One; Andrew Clark and George Nairn for permission to reproduce images in Cases One, Four and Eight; Percy Mather for the image used in Case Eight; Elizabeth Errington for the images used in Case Eleven; and Andria Raistrick for providing copies of the two marriage certificates and other material used in Case Twelve.

Also to Mike Barton, Chief Constable of Durham Constabulary, and Nick Cook, for writing their respective forewords; and my wife Kathryn for tolerating my absences caused by research and the need to visit scenes in order to provide photographs.

Please note that in exceptional circumstances some images have been reproduced without sanction of the original publisher, but only after exhausting all means of tracing and identifying them.

About the Author

Paul Heslop joined Newcastle upon Tyne City Police in 1965 (later amalgamated into Northumbria Police). He served his time on the beat, supervised by patrol sergeants and inspectors, when on-the-street contact with the public was an essential ingredient in policing. Thereafter he spent most of his career as a detective in the Northumbria and Hertfordshire forces, including service in the Regional Crime Squads in both, the latter involving the investigation of serious crime in London and the Home Counties. He retired from the force in 1995, and since then has become an established writer on such diverse subjects as health and safety in the workplace, walking and local history. He is the author of nine books to date, and has written about crime for newspapers and periodicals. He lives in the Lake District.

Falsehood after Falsehood

Sunderland, 1839

Suspect:	*Jacon Friedrich Ehlert*
Age:	*28*
Charge:	*Murder*
Sentence:	*Execution*

Keelman James Alderson spotted a body in the River Wear around midday on Thursday, 13 June 1839. The body was floating about thirty yards from the north shore of the river, not far from the bridge, and with the assistance of two men from the *Atlantic*, which was moored nearby, Alderson managed to raise the body which was tied to a large lump of limestone weighing over seven stone.

It was the body of a man wearing only a flannel shirt, stockings, and a cotton shirt. If the man's identity was a mystery, the cause of his death wasn't, as it was clear that he had been the victim of a brutal murder for his head had been smashed in by a hammer-like instrument. The manner of disposal suggests that his killer had hoped he would remain undiscovered.

Until the Victorian times, law enforcement in Sunderland had been the responsibility of the parish council who appointed 'Old Charlies', elderly men who patrolled the streets, to carry lanterns at night. Then, in 1837, the town's police force was established and this was the first murder that the Sunderland force had to deal with, two years later. But whether justice was done will forever be in doubt when you consider that of the two suspects one

Sunderland of old. Ships on the River Wear. (Reproduced by kind permission of Andrew Clark and George Nairn)

was convicted on the uncorroborated word of the other, when it might just as easily have been the other way around.

The murder enquiry was headed by Superintendent William Brown and his deputy, Inspector Bailes. After having the body removed to the workhouse at Monkwearmouth, the policemen made enquiries on the river, and at eight thirty that evening they boarded a Prussian vessel, the *Phoenix*, from Stettin (now Szczecin in modern-day Poland). The crew of six men spoke only German, but nevertheless were able to tell them that their captain, Johann Friedrich Berckholtz, had been taken ashore at 4.30 a.m. the previous day, a Wednesday, but had not returned to the vessel.

The ship's mate accompanied Brown and Bailes to the captain's cabin where they found 'the bed made up as if no one had slept in it'. On one of the pillows Brown saw a large bloodstain which appeared to have been recently sponged and was still damp. He examined the partition at the head of the bed finding bloodstains on that too, as well as on a towel that was hanging in the cabin. When Brown mentioned the blood the mate got up to go on deck, but the superintendent 'put his hand on him' and arrested him. The mate, identified as twenty-eight-year-old Jacob Frederich Ehlert from Barth, Prussia (now part of Germany), was wearing a brown jacket, waistcoat and a neckerchief, all of which had marks of blood on them, and the jacket looked as though it had recently been washed.

With some difficulty, due to the lack of interpreter, Brown questioned the other crew members and found that only two of them claimed to have known of Captain Berckholtz going ashore on Wednesday morning. One was Ehlert, who said that he had woken the captain at 4 a.m., and the other was Daniel Friedrick Muller, an eighteen-year-old second apprentice, who said that he had rowed the captain ashore. Muller and the rest of the crew were all arrested.

Brown examined the ship 'very minutely' from the captain's berth to the cabin window at the stern, finding 'smears and streaks of blood' throughout. He discovered a spot of blood the size of a penny on the top and bottom of the frame of the cabin window, as well as blood on a shutter to the window and the handles of the two fastening bolts, 'as if some person with a bloody hand had touched them'. On the frame was a splinter with a piece of red wool caught on it that corresponded with the shirt worn by Ehlert, the only one of the crew who wore a red shirt. Brown concluded that the body had been dragged from the cabin and put out of the window at the stern of the vessel.

The murdered man was identified as Captain Berckholtz by two members of the crew. He had been seen to board the *Phoenix* on Tuesday night, and Ehlert and Muller were the only people who said they had seen him since.

All six members of the crew appeared before the Sunderland magistrates on the Friday morning – even though none of them had been formally charged. Muller was brought before the court after his comrades, thus suggesting he was the main suspect because he had rowed the captain ashore. After hearing the evidence of police and the seamen of other ships, the magistrates remanded the crew in custody until the next day, but shortly afterwards they were informed that the first apprentice, nineteen-year-old Johann Gustav Weidemann, wished to make a statement and he was brought before the court.

Ehlert

Mueller

A caricature of Ehlert (left) and Muller. (Author's collection)

Weidemann told the magistrates that at four o'clock on Wednesday morning he saw Ehlert in the captain's cabin, attempting to wash the floor. Weidemann asked Ehlert where the captain was and his response was that he had gone to shore. He then went on to tell the court that at two o'clock on Wednesday afternoon the ship's cook, Johann Eichstadt, and Muller had quarrelled. Eichstadt had found six five-franc pieces on Muller and had asked him how he came by the money. Muller said Ehlert had given it to him, but Ehlert declared Muller had stolen it from his trunk, whereupon Eichstadt declared, 'The mate [Ehlert] is a liar, the money belongs to the captain, and I will keep it until the captain comes on board.' Ehlert had explained to Weidemann that the floor was wet because he had 'thrown a glass of water'. On finding that the captain was still absent on Thursday morning, Weidemann thought he had gone to Newcastle.

Having heard Weidemann's testimony, the magistrates were informed that Muller wished to make 'a full disclosure of the circumstances attendant on the horrid affair' as he was 'unable to bear the tortures of concealed guilt'. Muller appeared before the court and with 'the greatest firmness and composure' gave his account.

Muller said that he had the watch shift on the *Phoenix* between midnight and two o'clock on Wednesday morning, and that at half past one Ehlert came on deck carrying a hammer and asked him to go with him below. Muller was reluctant to leave his post and on asking why he was needed, the mate replied, 'You must come down'. Muller went below and Ehlert told him to hold a lantern. They went into the captain's cabin where Ehlert struck the captain, who was in bed, on the head with the hammer. Muller cried out, 'Mate, what are you doing?' and Ehlert took hold of him and stated, 'You must remain here.'

Muller continued his account to the magistrates:

The mate took the body out of bed and slung a rope around the neck. He put a pair of stockings on the body and a pair of trousers, and fetched a bag made of sail-cloth and drew it over the body. I attempted to get out but he would not let me. He said if I would not help him to put away the body he would kill me with a knife which he drew from his pocket. Ehlert said to me, 'You must help me. If you do not I will kill you, but if you do I will give you £300.' I went to the roof and the mate went with me and took the skylight off. He cut a long cord from the gear and went below again and tied it round the body and came on deck, and pulled it up the skylight, hand over hand. I did not help to lift the body out of the cabin. He threw the body over the stern. I heard it plunge into the water. He desired me to bring the boat around to the stern. When I got it round he came down into the boat and fastened the line to it. I attempted to get away but he held me back. I had to help him row the boat to the south side of the river. In pulling up the river the body lost off the trousers. The mate went on shore and brought a stone into the boat. The mate pulled the body so it was above water and tied the stone to it. He let the stone and body go into the water. We both returned to the ship. He told me to rest in my berth, where the crew were asleep. He called me at four o'clock, saying, loudly, 'Fred, you must set the captain on shore'. The others would have heard. I went to the boat and rowed then returned to the ship. He told me to say I had put the captain ashore on the north side. He said if I said anything he would murder me.

Muller's account depicted that he had played a coerced role in the murder of Captain Berckholtz, and that he had been unable to escape and had been threatened with death by Jacob Ehlert. At the inquest on 15 June the testimonies of other witnesses were heard.

Local policeman Sergeant Holmes said that at about noon on Thursday he was on patrol when a man ran up to him and said a body had been found in the river, and that two men in a boat had recovered it. He saw a stone in the boat which he said 'weighed upwards of a hundredweight', and it was obvious to him that the head injury had been the cause of death. He and the men endeavoured to carry the body with the stone but could not.

Surgeon William Dodd formally pronounced death and later said that he was 'struck with the shocking mutilation' of the forehead, declaring that 'the bones were smashed in'.

After being told he need not answer any questions that might incriminate him, Muller declared, 'I saw blood spurting about when the mate struck the captain with a hammer.'

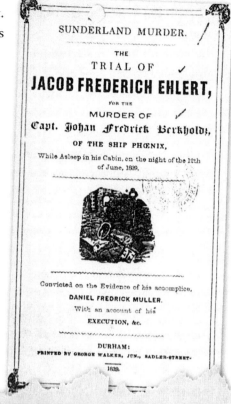

SUNDERLAND MURDER.

THE
TRIAL OF
JACOB FREDERICH EHLERT,
FOR THE
MURDER OF
Capt. Johan Fredrick Berkholds,
OF THE SHIP PHŒNIX,
While Asleep in his Cabin, on the night of the 12th of June, 1839.

Convicted on the Evidence of his accomplice,
DANIEL FREDRICK MULLER.
With an account of his
EXECUTION, &c.

DURHAM:
PRINTED BY GEORGE WALKER, JUN., SADLER-STREET.
1839.

A report into the murder of Captain Johann Friedrich Berckholtz. The spelling of foreign seamen's names varies in the documentation covering the case. (Author's collection)

A juryman asked him, 'Why did you refuse to go down into the cabin when the mate, your superior officer, called upon you?'

'I do not know,' replied Muller. 'The mate said I might go down to fetch some wine up.'

'Why did you not give the alarm during the two days which elapsed between the murder of the captain and the finding of his body?'

'Because I was afraid the mate would kill me,' replied Muller.

Jacob Ehlert was asked if he understood Muller's 'confession' or if he could explain why Muller had stated that Ehlert had 'given three blows to the captain's head'. Ehlert shook his head and declared, 'These are lies'. He also denied tying a rope about the captain and maintained that he had been in his own cabin before he met Muller at the top of the stairs rushing out of the captain's cabin. He claimed that at that point Muller had tried to leap overboard. Ehlert's solicitor, Mr Blech, said that his client wished to confront Muller, which the courtroom agreed to be 'right' and 'fair', so the witness was brought to appear before the magistrates.

'Who killed the captain?' asked Ehlert.

'You,' replied Muller.

'You are the murderer,' said Ehlert.

'You are the murderer,' said Muller.

More equally fruitless exchanges were made, and so Johann Eichstadt, the cook, was called upon to testify. He said that at four o'clock on Wednesday morning he had heard Ehlert calling to Muller, 'Fred, you have to set the captain ashore.' He also testified that on the Wednesday and Thursday Ehlert was wearing the captain's hat, and that on Wednesday evening Muller had been drinking; he searched Muller's berth and found spirits and some money in a box he had earlier seen on the captain's writing desk. It was French money – six five-franc pieces – and other small coins. He asked Muller about it, but he walked away. Eichstadt then went to Ehlert's berth and asked him where Muller could have got the money; he responded by laying his head on the table and he did not offer a reply. On Thursday afternoon Eichstadt was shown a body which he formally identified as the captain's.

The coroner summed up the inquest by telling the jury, 'I think, gentlemen, you will agree with me that the evidence is perfectly conclusive as to the guilt of the mate. The charge of murder is clearly brought home to him.' It was hardly conclusive at all, but the jury agreed and found Ehlert guilty of killing Captain Berckholtz, and committed him to the assizes for trial. All of the crew members were detained in custody. A few days later, Ehlert wrote to Superintendent Brown about his 'unhappy situation' of being accused of the cruel murder committed by the *jungmann* (Muller), which gave him the 'greatest pain' for he feared he would never confess. Captain Berckholtz was buried in St Peter's churchyard in Sunderland.

Elhert stood trial at Durham Assizes in July, before Justice Coltman, where he pleaded 'not guilty'. Daniel Muller appeared as a prosecution witness, and his testimony was long and precise. As well as reiterating what he had said before, he denied ever touching the captain's body 'from first to last', and on the issue of why he did not attempt an escape from Elhert when he went on shore to get the heavy stone, Muller said, 'The stone was so near the boat that the mate had one foot in the boat and the other on the land.'

Mr Knowles, defending, said the jury were required upon the evidence of one witness to find Ehlert guilty, and that the testimony held little weight because Muller was an accomplice and, therefore, as equally guilty. It was only because Muller had got the head start and turned King's Evidence that he was allowed to give his evidence on oath, while the prisoner could not – accused persons were not allowed to testify in their own defence at that time.

Knowles went on to say that Muller had, by his own account, been asked by Ehlert to go down to the captain's cabin, saying, 'I thought the mate had wanted me to bring up some wine.' Muller, it seemed, wanted the jury to believe that Ehlert deliberately chose to have a witness to his murder of Captain Berckholtz. For what purpose would he call him down to witness the murder? Not for assistance for he had none, according to Muller. Knowles declared that the only safe course was for the jury to reject Muller's unreliable evidence altogether. Knowles went on to say:

Muller said he wanted to get away, but Ehlert stopped him. He went upstairs, leaving Ehlert alone in the cabin.

Captain Berckholtz's gravestone in St Peter's churchyard, Monkwearmouth (© Paul Heslop)

Muller's companions were within a few feet of him; the slightest cry would have woken them. Muller asserted that the mate said he would have £300. So is he saying Ehlert would commit the murder but he, Muller, was to have the money? There was the story about the body being brought up through the skylight. Muller said he never touched the body, and he gave no assistance. Yet even the prosecution say one person could not raise it without assistance. Muller said he 'brought the boat around'. Why did he not go away then? He says he did not wish to betray the mate! This is so inconsistent it is impossible for a human being to believe. There is falsehood after falsehood in every story Muller has told.

Muller said Ehlert told him to pretend to put the captain onshore, that he was away a quarter of an hour. What was to prevent him getting away then? A few strokes of the oars and he is on shore, the mate with his knife still on the ship. Instead he rows to the south shore and comes back and says nothing. And when they were all taken into custody, why did he not tell the police that Ehlert had murdered the captain? Instead, he told the police he put the captain on shore!

The judge said it was impossible to regard Muller in any other light than as a willing accomplice and that his testimony was to be heard with great caution. One could also say that his dubious evidence was the *only* evidence against Ehlert, and that without it there was no proof of his guilt. Both men, said his Lordship, were in this together – but only one stood charged with the murder, and it was in respect of him, and him alone, that the jury had to return a verdict. They took just eight minutes to declare that their verdict was 'Guilty'.

The judge addressed Ehlert, saying, 'You have taken the life of a man whom you were bound to protect from violence and harm.' He sentenced him to death 'in the usual form', saying his body was to be buried within the precincts of the prison. Ehlert was duly removed – still protesting his innocence.

At 8 a.m. on Friday 16 August, Jacob Frederich Ehlert was taken from his cell in Durham Gaol to be publicly executed. Facing imminent death, it was reported that Ehlert displayed 'a remarkable degree of fortitude'. Asked if he willingly gave up his own life for the life he had taken, he replied in German, 'No. I have taken no life at all.'

The unnamed executioner was described as 'an old practitioner with a sharp, cunning eye'. He was dressed in a suit of coarse grey cloth and wearing a striped woollen nightcap, and a blue and white spotted handkerchief tied around his face. The reason for this strange attire is neither explained nor apparent. Pinioning Ehlert, he placed a white cap over his head and led him out to the scaffold where, having placed the rope about his neck, he withdrew the bolt. Watched by the crowd, Ehlert fell several feet and hung without any struggle; it seemed life was extinct. But then he began to 'manifest agonies of death': his feet appeared to seek a resting place; he attempted to reach upwards, but in vain. He twisted and turned for eight minutes before, at last, his

How Ehlert's executioner was portrayed in the Daily Journal. (Author's collection)

contortions ceased. It was reported that his last statement was that Muller struck the blow that killed Captain Berckholtz, and that he had screened the deed 'from motives of humanity'. The general expression emanating from the crowd was that Muller should have been hanged with him.

Perhaps he should have, but the prosecution's difficulty was obvious. There was no witness to the crime other than the two men who were present – the mate and the young apprentice. Had both been charged, the judge would have been obliged to warn the jury of the danger of accepting the evidence of an accomplice, and with no independent evidence forthcoming, both may have been acquitted. But using one as a witness allowed the conviction of the other as sole perpetrator. They might just have readily used Ehlert as the witness and proceeded against Muller, the murder of the captain would have been solved just the same. Even so, the front page of an official report into the crime describes Ehlert as being 'Convicted on the Evidence of his accomplice, Muller'. It seems Muller, who was the first to speak out before the examining magistrates, was accepted as the witness the prosecution needed. Ehlert, of course, was not permitted to say anything at all.

SOLVED

A Catalogue of Death

West Auckland & Beyond, 1852-72

Suspect:	Mary Ann Cotton
Age:	40
Charge:	Murder
Sentence:	Execution

Mary Ann Cotton was a Sunday school teacher, a dressmaker, respected nurse and pathological killer by the time she was forty, when she was hanged for the murder of her stepson in 1872.

She was born Mary Ann Robson at Low Moorsley, near Hetton-le-Hole, in 1832, the daughter of a coal-mine sinker. Shortly afterwards, the Robson family moved to nearby East Rainton and later to Murton. A miner's work was hard and dangerous, and life for mining families was grim indeed by today's standards. Mary Ann was only nine when her father, Michael Robson, died tragically at the pit; he was only thirty years old.

Mary Ann went to the local Wesleyan Chapel Sunday school and later took her own class there. At sixteen she was a nursemaid to a family at South Hetton and then a dressmaker. In July 1854, she married a labourer named William Mowbray at the Newcastle register office which was located some distance away, suggesting that she was pregnant at the time. The newlyweds moved to Cornwall, but four years later they returned to County Durham with a child, also called Mary Ann. Mary Ann senior told friends that she had had four other children in Cornwall and that they had all died, which was not uncommon in Victorian times. However, the following catalogue of death of both children and adults, almost all of which can be ascribed to Mary Ann, was hardly down to grim social conditions and lack of medical expertise.

On 5 April 1857 the Mowbrays had another daughter, Margaret Jane, but the little girl was dead before 1861. In 1860, Mary Ann junior died aged four; the cause of death was put down to gastric fever. Another daughter born in 1861 was also called Margaret Jane. The Mowbrays then moved to South Hetton, where a fourth daughter named Isabella was born. In 1863, Mary Ann and William had a baby boy that they named John Robert, and following his birth the family moved to Sunderland. Sadly, John Robert was dead within the year.

In January 1865, William Mowbray died aged forty-seven, his death was also ascribed to gastric fever. At that time Mary Ann was thirty-two with two surviving children, Margaret Jane and Isabella. She collected £35 in insurance money from the Prudential in respect of the death of her husband. She and the children then moved to Seaham Harbour, where she took a room next to the Lord Seaham Inn, now the Harbour View Hotel. Here she met Joseph Nattrass, who was engaged to a local girl but had a relationship with Mary Ann. He married his fiancé nonetheless and moved to Shildon, near Bishop Auckland. (Nattrass would again feature in Mary Ann's life at a later date.)

In April 1865, Mary Ann's youngest child, Margaret Jane died, aged three, also allegedly of gastric fever. Isabella, then aged six, went to live with her grandmother, leaving Mary Ann on her own. Mary Ann then worked in the Sunderland Infirmary Fever House, where she favourably impressed the doctors and became acquainted with one of the patients, George Ward, a man of her own age. On 28 August 1865, Ward and Mary Ann were married at St Peter's Church, Monkwearmouth – the first of three church wedding ceremonies she would attend.

Mary Ann bore no children to Ward, who later that year became ill. His unnamed illness perplexed several doctors and he was dead by October the following year, his death being ascribed to 'fever' – he was thirty-three.

The following month, James Robinson applied for a housekeeper when his wife Hannah died at Pallion (a part of Sunderland). It was hardly surprising that he needed help in the home, as he had five children to bring up. Mary

Ann got the job and was part of the Robinson household before the year was out. Just three weeks after the death of his mother and one week after Mary Ann's arrival in the family home, ten-month-old John Robinson was dead, evidently another victim of gastric fever.

The following March, Mary Ann was pregnant by Robinson. She was then called away to look after her mother, who died unexpectedly nine days later, allowing Mary Ann to return to the Robinson household. Mary Ann's oldest surviving child, Isabella, returned with Mary Ann, with fatal consequences; she died on 2 May. Robinson's son James, aged six, and Elizabeth, aged eight, perished about the same time. All three children reportedly died of gastric fever. By this time a senior policeman, Superintendent Henderson, and three of Robinson's sisters suspected Mary Ann of being a poisoner. Henderson wanted the children's bodies exhumed but, for whatever reason, this did not happen.

The Harbour View Hotel, Seaham Harbour. Formerly the Lord Seaham Inn. Mary Ann Cotton took a room next door after the death of her first husband, William Mowbray. (© Paul Heslop)

Robinson stood by Mary Ann, and even married her at Bishopwearmouth Church on 11 August 1867. He and Mary Ann became the parents of a little girl, Mary Isabella, that November. The baby died the following March – of gastric fever.

A total of five children died whilst Mary Ann was living with Robinson. Robinson would not insure his own life, although Mary Ann collected an insurance payment in respect of Isabella, her daughter by Mowbray. Undaunted by Robinson's refusal to insure his life, she attempted to do it for him without his knowledge, but unfortunately for her and mercifully for him, he found out and prevented a course of action that would surely have had fatal consequences for him. In any event, his time with Mary Ann was drawing to a close due to her criminal activity.

James Robinson had two building society accounts. In early 1869, it was discovered that there were some forged entries regarding payments into one of them, and it seemed that someone was inserting additional payments of 10s

St Peter's Church, Monkwearmouth, where Mary Ann Cotton married George Ward – husband number two. (© Paul Heslop)

(which suggested there was more money in the account than was the case). The society threatened action, but Mary Ann falsely told her husband that the society did not, after all, want the monies made up. He then discovered that she had been trying to acquire a loan of £5 by giving the names of Robinson's brother-in-law and uncle as guarantors without their knowledge. When Robinson's son told him that Mary Ann had been sending him to the pawnbrokers, she fled the household with their surviving child, and the hapless Robinson found himself in £7 arrears with the other building society – presumably money now in his wife's possession. He never had anything more to do with her again.

At the end of that year, Mary Ann and the child called on a friend in Sunderland. She told the friend that she needed to pop out to post a letter and never returned, leaving the child behind. The fortunate child (whose life was probably not insured) was returned to James Robinson.

Mary Ann had been married three times, widowed twice and had left her third husband. Alone again she would have sought another husband, a breadwinner, and by early 1870 she had identified one. Frederick Cotton was a coal miner living at North Walbottle, a mining village west of Newcastle. She was introduced to him by his sister, Margaret, whom Mary Ann knew

North Walbottle Colliery, near Newcastle, where Frederick Cotton worked. (Author's collection)

from her time of being in service. By that time Mary Ann was working as a laundry maid at Stanhope Rectory in Weardale.

Frederick Cotton lived with his wife, Adelaide, and their four children, two boys and two girls. Adelaide died in January 1870, along with the Cottons' second daughter, both of typhus fever. These deaths had nothing to do with Mary Ann, but she was visiting the Cotton household when the other daughter and Frederick's sister, Margaret, allegedly died of pneumonia. By then Mary Ann and Frederick were lovers, so one must wonder about Margaret's death and whether Mary Ann thought she was in the way. By April Mary Ann was pregnant, presumably by Frederick Cotton, and Robert Robson Cotton was born the following January. Also still living were the last of Frederick Cotton's children, Frederick Cotton Junior and Charles Edward Cotton.

By this time, thirteen out of fourteen children were dead, as well as two of Mary Ann's husbands, and two other adults had perished. Most seemed to have died of gastric fever, with symptoms such as diarrhoea and vomiting, and were likely to have been in excruciating pain. These are also the symptoms of death caused by arsenic poisoning, but despite some suspicion, Mary Ann remained at liberty to continue a lifestyle that allowed her to live with unsuspecting people, including children.

Mary Ann went to Spennymoor, where she was employed as housekeeper by a Dr Heffernan. However, by July 1870 she had returned to North Walbottle, and on 17 September she and Frederick Cotton were bigamously married at St Andrew's Church, Newcastle upon Tyne.

Another church wedding. St Andrew's Church, Newcastle upon Tyne. Mary Ann married Frederick Cotton here, bigamously, on 17th September 1870. (© Paul Heslop)

Afterwards, she completed two insurance forms with the Prudential in respect of Frederick Cotton's two boys by his previous marriage.

By summer the following year Mary Ann, Frederick Cotton, their son Robert Robson Cotton and Cotton's own two sons by his previous wife, had moved to yet another location – West Auckland, in south-west Durham. She was thirty-nine years old.

The Cottons moved into Johnson Terrace and Frederick went to work at the local pit, but not for long. He died suddenly on 19 September 1871 of gastric fever, said the doctor. Three months later, Mary Ann's former lover, miner Joseph Nattrass, moved into the house ostensibly as a lodger. Then Mary Ann, the former nurse, was asked to look after Mr Quick-Manning, an excise officer at the local brewery who had smallpox. Quick-Manning was of considerable social standing, higher than a miner. He was also free, as was Mary Ann, and they became lovers. She would have wanted him for a husband but there was the matter of her three children and Nattrass, which would have been a barrier to marriage, at least for Quick-Manning. It was a barrier Mary Ann quickly removed.

In the space of just three weeks, there were three deaths in the Cotton household. The first was Mary Ann's stepson Frederick Cotton, aged ten, who apparently died of fever. Then Mary Ann's own son, Robert Robson Cotton, who died aged just fourteen months, apparently through convulsions caused by teething. His death was followed by that of Joseph Natrass, also apparently of fever. Only one child, seven-year-old Charles Edward Cotton remained. When she fell pregnant to Quick-Manning she would have felt optimistic about the future: snaring the excise officer who would surely marry the mother of his child-to-be, although her stepson may have still been in the way. If she considered him to be, there was a remedy. But before expediting it, Mary Ann and Charles Edward moved to nearby Front Street, a three-storeyed house with one room on each floor. The house still stands today.

On Saturday, 6 July 1872, Thomas Riley, the assistant overseer at West Auckland, called to enquire if Mary Ann could look after a smallpox victim. She explained that unfortunately she was unable to help because she had to look after Charles Edward, her stepson. In fact, she told Riley, he could help her by making an order to have Charles Edward placed into the workhouse as he was not actually her child. Riley said he could only do so if she went with him and Mary Ann declined.

'I have heard you might marry,' said Riley.

'It might be so,' she replied, 'but the boy is in the way.' Then she added, 'Perhaps it won't matter, as I won't be troubled long. He'll go like all the rest of the Cotton family.' Six days later, as Riley was passing, he saw Mary Ann at the cottage door. 'My boy's dead,' she told him. Riley went to see a policeman, Sergeant Thomas Hutchinson.

Riley also went to see Dr Kilburn, who was surprised at the news as he had seen the boy the previous day, and he postponed making out a death certificate. This was a blow to Mary Ann, who needed the certificate to claim the £4 10s (around £381 today) insurance money from the Prudential's agent. Sergeant Hutchinson reported the case to the coroner who then ordered an inquest. It was held the following day in the pub next to Mary Ann's house, but they could scarcely have expected to ascertain a cause of death as Doctors Kilburn and Chalmers had only began their post-mortem examination an hour before the inquest started – bizarrely, we might think today, on a table in Mary Ann's house. There was no opportunity of making an immediate chemical examination of the contents of stomach or organs. In any event, Dr Kilburn believed death could have been due to gastroenteritis; he told the inquest jury so and death through natural causes was recorded. Charles Edward was buried, Mary Ann got her death certificate and that, it seemed, was that.

But Mary Ann would have been mortified if she had known

The house in West Auckland where Mary Ann Cotton murdered her stepson. The house still stands today. (© Paul Heslop, 2012)

what Dr Kilburn had done. After the hasty post-mortem, he took the viscera home, where he poured the contents into a jar and buried the rest in his garden. He then submitted the contents of the jar to a Reinsch test; one can imagine his feelings when he discovered the tell-tale deposit of arsenic on the copper plate. The following day Mary Ann was arrested.

On 26 July, young Charles Edward's remains were exhumed, and the police also dug up the remains of the viscera from Dr Kilburn's garden. Dr Thomas Scattergood, an expert in forensic medicine and toxicology, found arsenic in the stomach contents and bowels, as well as in the liver, lungs, heart, kidneys and faeces, the latter having been preserved by a suspicious neighbour, Mary Ann Dodds, who was in the Cotton household when Charles Edward died.

On 21 August, Mary Ann appeared before the Bishop Auckland magistrates. John Townend, a chemist, said a little boy, whose name he did not know, had come into his shop on 27 May asking for soft soap and arsenic, but he refused to serve him. Five minutes later Mrs Dodds came in, saying Mrs Cotton had sent her and she bought between a half to one ounce of arsenic. She confirmed that Charles Edward had earlier tried to buy the arsenic in Townend's shop. (Anyone could purchase arsenic at that time because it was common practice to add it to soft soap and rub the mixture on a bedstead to kill bugs.) Dr Scattergood told the court that he had found more than half a grain of white arsenic in Charles Edward's stomach and he declared that death was due to arsenic poisoning. Asked if she wished to say anything, Mary Ann simply replied, 'No.'

Three more bodies were exhumed from the churchyard at St Helen Auckland. Dr Scattergood found almost eighteen grains of arsenic in Nattrass' stomach and other organs, confirming that this was the cause of death. Two others, Frederick Cotton junior and the baby, Robert Robson Cotton, both died from arsenic poisoning too. They sought to exhume the body of Frederick Cotton senior, but they were unable to locate the coffin among graves 'thick as furrows in a field'. Regardless, Mary Ann was charged with three more murders.

As for Nattrass, their neighbour, Phoebe Robson, had seen him 'bad in the bowels' and having fits. He was in agony and had to be held down by Mary Ann. 'He clashed his head against the wall and bedpost and bent his toes as if in cramp,' Mrs Robson said. She had seen Mary Ann pouring tea from two teapots, his and hers presumably. Mary Ann had also been seen giving Frederick tea. On the Wednesday before Frederick died, he asked Elizabeth Atkinson if her husband, Elijah, could pray with him. He asked for his cap, and was still wearing it when his body was exhumed. Robert Robson Cotton, Mary Ann's own son, was just fourteen months old. Mary Ann was seen kneeling by his cradle, even as Nattrass was dying close by. Yet none of the doctors who attended considered foul play.

Mary Ann Cotton stood trial at Durham Assizes in March 1873, before Justice Archibald. She denied the charge of murdering her stepson, Charles Edward Cotton, with the remaining cases being left on file. Charles Russell led the prosecution and Campbell Foster defended Mary Ann, who appeared 'depressed, careworn and anxious'. Russell said that Mary Ann had poisoned her stepson, who was seven years old. His life, and others, had been insured with the Prudential Assurance Company, and that Mary Ann received payment on the death of the insured, which Russell declared was the motive for the crime.

The evidence was circumstantial, as no one actually witnessed Mary Ann administering the poison, which was expected in a crime such as this; however, she was known to have acquired arsenic. Campbell Foster suggested the administration of arsenic had been accidental, or that if it was deliberate there was no proof that Mary Ann was responsible. He even suggested arsenic could be inhaled from wallpaper. Dr Scattergood said he had never heard of anyone dying of such a cause and that arsenic in the stomach implied recent administration.

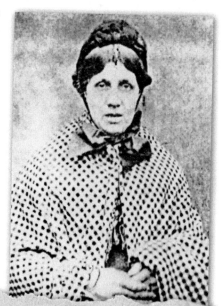

Campbell Foster said the evidence in the three other cases was inadmissible, as Mary Ann had not been indicted with these. 'A mother could not give her own child [Robert Robson Cotton] arsenic,' he said. The judge told the jury that the

Mary Ann Cotton. This photograph was probably taken when she was on remand in Durham Gaol. (Author's collection)

prosecution was entitled to draw attention to the other deaths, and that in all cases arsenic had been administered. When the jury found Mary Ann guilty of the murder of Charles Edward Cotton 'a deathly pallor overspread her face', and she whispered, even then, that she was not guilty. His Lordship told her, 'You seem to [think] that you could carry out your wicked crimes without detection.' When he sentenced her to death, she 'almost slipped into unconsciousness'.

Mary Ann Cotton's execution at Durham Gaol was set for 8 a.m. on Monday, 24 March 1873. Five days earlier, the baby daughter she had in prison was taken from her. She never confessed to killing her stepson or anyone else. She was not without public sympathy, however. Martha Olive, of Dorchester, wrote to the Home Secretary: 'I have just heard with extreme horror that the poor woman Cotton is to be executed. Can it really be possible that there can be a law that would take the life of a young mother who has a suckling child?' The Home Secretary was unmoved, whilst the *Durham County Advertiser* wrote, 'The best thing for society and Mary Ann was that she should quit the earth'.

Mary Ann's hangman was William Calcraft who, despite his forty-five years' experience in the job, was always allowing a 'short drop', whereby the subject of his endeavours would drop a short distance and be left to slowly strangle in agony, instead of falling an adequate distance to facilitate a quick death. This was Mary Ann's fate, one seen as fitting by many, including the *Newcastle Daily Chronicle*: 'Here was the vengeance of the penal code, Christian England demanding an eye for an eye, ache for ache, gripe for gripe, pang for pang, torture for torture'.

'Heaven is my home,' Mary Ann had whispered as she waited for the imminent arrival of her executioner.

Her usual motive for murder was money, although in the case of Charles Edward it was probably to get him out of the way so that she could tempt Quick-Manning into marriage. Others she killed for reasons that suited her. It is worth noting that the only husband whose life was not insured, James Robinson, survived.

It is likely that she avoided detection because she never stayed in one place long enough to arouse suspicions, although with the sheer number of lives lost she did not escape suspicion altogether. Those whose deaths may be ascribed to her are: her first husband William Mowbray and all eight of their children;

her second husband, George Ward; her mother; her third husband's three children (although James Robinson himself escaped death), and the first of her own children by him; Frederick Cotton and his sister, Margaret, and his two sons, including Charles Edward, the murder of whom she was convicted; her son to Frederick Cotton, Robert Robson Cotton, and her lover, Joseph Nattrass. Of the twelve children she bore, only two survived – the child she had by Robinson, who was returned to him, and the daughter she bore by Quick-Manning, born in prison. Some of her earlier children may have died through natural causes, but we cannot know for sure.

Her victims, every one, died in unspeakable agony. Those who saw her dying children spoke of them 'rolling about in bed' and 'frothing at the mouth'. Blood relation or otherwise, it meant nothing to Mary Ann. Anyone in the way, or whose death would provide insurance money, was doomed.

As for the excise officer, Quick-Manning, he was fortunate indeed not to perish, as he surely would have if he had married Mary Ann Cotton and fulfilled a husband's duty to take out life insurance.

'The West Auckland Poisoning Case' showing: Mary Ann Cotton (centre) though not as she actually appeared; St Helen's Church, St Helen Auckland (top); Mary Ann's house in Front Street, West Auckland (bottom right); Sergeant Thomas Hutchinson to whom Dr Kilburn reported finding arsenic in Charles Edward Cotton's remains (bottom left). (Author's collection)

SOLVED

A Factional Dispute

Darlington, 1875

Suspect:	*James Durkin, James Flynn, Michael Gilligan*
Age:	*33, 21, 22*
Charge:	*Murder and Manslaughter*
Sentence:	*Execution and fifteen years' penal servitude*

Forty-two-year-old Irishman John Kilcran was a bricklayer's labourer living in Darlington, and like most working men he liked a drink at the weekend. So it was on Easter Sunday, 28 March 1875 that Kilcran enjoyed a pint of ale with his friend, Patrick Riley, at the Plough Inn in Parkgate where Riley lived. They then enjoyed a glass of rum in the nearby Lord Nelson Inn after which they parted, with Kilcran setting off alone for his home in Church Street, just a few minutes' walk away.

A short time later, at 9.50 p.m., John William Rickaby and Charles Oyston happened to be standing in Parkgate when they saw seven men approaching. Two of the men crossed the road and looked intently at both Rickaby and Oyston for a moment, before rejoining their companions. The group continued to the end of Park Street where they stopped to fasten their coats. Just then, John Kilcran, arrived in Parkgate and was crossing the road when he was approached by the group.

Rickaby and Oyston saw one of the men punch Kilcran in the face, then another step forward and, taking something from his trousers pocket, his hand 'shot out' against Kilcran's face. Rickaby and Oyston heard what appeared to be the sound of a pistol. Kilcran fell to the ground immediately, calling out, 'Oh, I am done!' Another man kicked him. Rickaby saw the man who had taken the object from his pocket place it back there, before the man walked off in the direction of the Lord Nelson Inn. Charles Oyston helped take Kilcran home.

This seemingly unprovoked attack may have appeared to have been randomly chosen on a hapless passer-by, delivered for no other reason than that of spite, or perhaps through drunkenness. However, John Kilcran was the local secretary of the Hibernian Society, and his assailants, it would transpire, were members of the Fenians. Their common cause of independence of British rule did not unite the two Irish factions on that night, and the violence that spilled onto the streets of Darlington would result in cold-blooded murder, when John Kilcran died of his injuries eleven days later.

Ellen McCabe was also in Parkgate that evening. At 9.50 p.m., having stopped to talk to sisters Sarah and Margaret Burnside, she saw seven men walking towards Park Street. The streetlight on the corner was lit, and she recognised six of them. The group included thirty-three-year-old James Durkin, twenty-one-year-old James Flynn and twenty-two-year-old Michael Gilligan, three Irish labourers who lived in the town. She saw Durkin enter the Malt Shovel Inn, then the Lord Nelson Inn, while his companions stood and waited. The men stood about forty yards away and waited until Durkin rejoined them. McCabe then heard the sound of a blow, followed by a groan. Shouting 'Murder!' she ran towards Park Street, where she saw Durkin leaning over Kilcran, before all seven of the group disappeared.

Sarah and Margaret Burnside also saw the group of men. They saw Durkin go into the Malt Shovel and Lord Nelson inns. When he emerged from the latter, both women heard him say to another member of the group, 'He's not there'. They too heard the sound of a groan, and saw Charles Oyston help to pick Kilcran up off the ground.

At that time, a man named Iceton was standing in Park Street with a male companion when they saw the same group of men approaching. Iceton said to his companion that they had better move on in case the group set upon them. They remained where they were, however, and Iceton saw Kilcran approaching, then one of the men from the group hit him in the face. A second man then stepped forward and struck Kilcran on the head with 'some instrument', knocking him to the ground, whereupon the men kicked him. At the sound of 'Murder!' the men made off. A man named Iceton helped Kilcran to his feet, and he and Oyston took him home. Dr Howison was called to attend the wounded man.

Just before ten o'clock, Police Constable Richard Ianson was on patrol and saw Michael Gilligan approaching from the direction of Park Street. He noticed that Gilligan, whom he knew, was walking 'rather quickly'. The constable went to Park Street where he was told there had been 'a row'. Meanwhile, Dr James Howison examined Kilcran, who had sustained a large wound to his forehead from the left eyebrow upwards, about three inches long. The doctor regarded the wound to be serious and considered Kilcran unlikely to survive, even though he was conscious and able to speak.

PC Ianson's enquiries also led him to the home of Kilcran, who named one of his assailants as James Flynn, and further enquiries revealed the name of James Durkin. These men were known to the police. Flynn, Durkin and Gilligan were all arrested by PC Ianson at 11.45 that evening.

On Wednesday morning, 31 March, the three prisoners appeared before the Darlington magistrates, charged with assaulting John Kilcran. The court was told of Kilcran's injuries, and that it was not known if he would recover.

The case was adjourned on the Wednesday, and at court again on the Friday, Iceton said the man who had first struck Kilcran in the face was

Darlington, c. 1900. (Reproduced by kind permission of Crown Street Library, Darlington)

not among the prisoners, but when asked if the man who struck the second blow was, he replied, 'Yes, Gilligan is the man.' He did not see the others do anything, but they were only three or four yards away and offered Kilcran 'no assistance'. Iceton said Kilcran was bleeding heavily when he helped him to his feet, and that he saw no instrument on the ground.

Kilcran, of course, was unable to attend court, so the case was adjourned again. He was unconscious and not expected to live, said the prosecution. He died at home at four o'clock the following Thursday, 8 April. The *Northern Echo* reported that 'The parties concerned are all Irishmen, and it is supposed the unfortunate deceased met his death through faction disputes'. However, the *Echo* failed to remind its readers that on Saturday night, 27 March, the day prior to the attack, another man named Henry Stephens, who lodged at Patrick Riley's beerhouse (the Plough Inn), was attacked in Parkgate by a party of men. He was set upon on his way home, without provocation, and was severely beaten. James McCabe, another Irishman, had been arrested for the assault, which was said to have arisen because McCabe was a member of the Hibernian Society and Stephens was a Fenian.

James McCabe was the brother of Ellen McCabe, a witness in the Kilcran case and who had, along with her friends, identified Michael Gilligan as being at the scene when Kilcran was assaulted. A Fenian allegedly assaulted by a Hibernian on Saturday, and a Hibernian allegedly assaulted by a Fenian on Sunday. Was Ellen McCabe's testimony honestly given?

The Fenian Movement sought independence for Ireland and believed that the only way to achieve this was through violence against the British state. The political implications of those times are too complex for inclusion here; suffice to say that they fervently believed in their cause. The Hibernian Movement shared similar goals, forming secret societies in Ireland, with the 'avowed purpose' to protect the Roman Catholic Church and clergy. One movement was secular, the other religious. Whatever the issues, their bitter rivalry spilled onto the streets of Darlington. On 10 April, the *Echo* reported: 'The circumstances surrounding the crime are of a peculiarly significant character to our Irish population, proving the lamentable fact that party feeling and party outrages have not yet disappeared from among us ... The obvious inference is that we have now added to our list of local Irish party outrages another murder'.

A post-mortem examination on Kilcran was carried out by Dr Howison and he reported his findings at the inquest, beginning with his initial visit to

Kilcran's home on the night that he was attacked. He had found a contused wound on the forehead through the left eyebrow, corresponding with a fracture of the skull. The skull was depressed, he said, and the wound could not have been caused by a hand without anything in it. 'The fracture of the skull would make a crack, as loud as a pistol being fired,' said Howison, adding that he was surprised Kilcran lived so long. The post-mortem showed that the instrument that caused the puncture to the skull had penetrated the membrane and gone 'some distance' into the brain – 'about an inch', he said. Howison gave the cause of death as injury to the brain through the compound fracture of the skull. He concluded by saying a knuckle duster or spike may have caused the injury.

Ellen McCabe was among those who testified at the inquest. After reiterating her evidence given at the earlier magistrates hearing, she was asked if she saw a woman called Margaret Glaney on the night in question. She replied that she did not. The relevance of the question soon became apparent, but not before PC Ianson told the court that Flynn and Durkin had denied 'cutting' Kilcran, and Gilligan had told him that he had been in the company of a man named Charles Geldert, helping him to attend to horses at Michael Watson's stables. He said he had not seen Kilcran that night, and that he 'had never touched him'.

Margaret Glaney lived in Park Street, Darlington. She said that on the night in question she was going home, close to ten o'clock, when, nearing the Lord Nelson Inn, she met James Durkin. She had asked him if he had been to see his father. 'Yes,' Durkin replied, and she said that he then walked in the direction of Parkgate with her. Glaney claimed that halfway along Parkgate they heard a crack, and that they ran, only to find Kilcran lying in the middle of the road. There was no one else around. When questioned, she admitted she was Durkin's stepsister, and although she wasn't actually asked if she was lying to provide him with an alibi, the question may have been superfluous.

The coroner summed up by saying John Kilcran had been attacked by seven men, 'who acted upon some concerted plan', and that one struck him with a sharp instrument with a spike and that the resulting wound killed him. Three witnesses – Rickaby, Oyston and Iceton – spoke with certainty that Gilligan struck the fatal blow. It is hardly surprising that the jury's verdict was 'Wilful Murder' when the coroner repeated that 'Gilligan committed the act'. Gilligan, who turned 'ghastly pale' on hearing the verdict, replied in a low voice, 'I am innocent'. The prisoners were committed to be tried at the next assizes, and John Kilcran's remains were interred in Darlington's West Cemetery.

Michael Gilligan, James Durkin and James Flynn stood trial at the Durham Assizes in July. Gilligan stood for the murder of John Kilcran, and Durkin and Flynn for aiding and abetting. All three pleaded 'not guilty'.

Charles Oyston and John Rickaby reiterated their earlier evidence. Kilcran was bleeding 'fearfully' from his brow, said Oyston. He said the lamp on the corner was lit on what was a 'bright night' and that he knew Gilligan well enough by sight, if not by name, and he could confirm that it was he who struck the fatal blow. He testified that he didn't see Durkin or Flynn 'do anything'. Rickaby had seen Gilligan before and saw him strike Kilcran with something that he had in his hand. When the counsel, Mr Blackwell, asked if he would know a man again if he had seen him before, Rickaby replied, 'If you should come up to me I should know you if I saw you again.' The judge was quick to suppress the inevitable laughter that ensued.

Sarah and Margaret Burnside both said Durkin had visited the two public houses and when he emerged had declared to a friend, 'He's not there.' It could be supposed that they were looking for Kilcran.

PC Ianson said that he knew all of the prisoners, and just before ten o'clock on the night in question had seen Gilligan coming from the direction of Parkgate. When he had spoken to him about wounding Kilcran, Gilligan had replied, 'I'd never seen him tonight. I never touched him. I was helping a man called Charles Geldart to do my cousin Mick's horses.' Ianson searched Gilligan at the police station and found nothing, but Gilligan had had every opportunity to discard a weapon and so the lack of one did not prove his innocence. There is no mention of the police searching the streets for a weapon. PC Ianson, questioned by Mr Blackwell, said he had known Gilligan about two years and knew 'nothing against him'.

Mr Edge, for the prosecution, summed up, saying that the jury could come to no other conclusion than Michael Gilligan had killed John Kilcran. Mr Blackwell said he had never heard evidence so slight as that against him; PC Ianson had said he knew of no previous convictions against the suspect and had not even seen him with Kilcran, or with the other two men. Yet the jury were to come to the conclusion that he was guilty of murder 'simply on the evidence of two or three witnesses'. Mr Edge then went on to ask,

'Because the man belongs to the sister country, dear old Ireland, was he to be a murderer?' There was absence of motive, he said, before asserting that Gilligan 'could not be the man' whom PC Ianson, 'who was a truthful officer', saw that night. Mr Skidmore, Durkin and Flynn's defence, said that the evidence was flimsy and weak.

The judge said nothing could justify the use of a weapon, and that whoever had used it was guilty of murder. The jury retired for just fifteen minutes before returning to the courtroom, where the foreman declared: 'We find Micheal Gilligan guilty of murder.' They found Durkin and Flynn both guilty of manslaughter. A plea for mercy on account of previous good character was entered in respect of Gilligan.

Asked why sentence of death should not be passed, Gilligan said:

I went on Easter Sunday night to help my cousin Michael to do up his horses, then I went to sell some tickets for a concert in the Livingstone Hall. As I came along Park Street I saw some men but I did not pass any remarks to them. During the six years I have been in Darlington I have seen many a row there, and many a fight, both connected with McCabe's and Riley's. I never interfered with them, nor them with me. As I stand before my God I swear they brought witnesses to swear my life away. I was going to bed when Ianson came in. I told him I had not assaulted the man. I take God as my judge that I went home quietly that night, and I was never the cause of any quarrel. When I was before the [coroner's] jury the superintendent presented it as an Irish row. May the cries of my wife and two children be upon them. I swear I am innocent.

At this point his voice faltered and he stopped talking.

His Lordship, 'labouring under great emotion', said, 'I am satisfied from the evidence that jury reached a proper verdict. You committed a fellow man into the other world without the least chance of preparation, but more consideration will be offered you than you gave him. You will have the advantage in prison of spiritual advice. I implore you to throw away any hope of mercy and prepare yourself for the crime you committed by death on the scaffold.'

Durkin said he took no part in the 'row', saying he had no ill-feeling against Kilcran. He said Kilcran was 'always fighting' and that Gilligan did not strike him, that one of the men not arrested was the man who struck him.

Flynn merely declared that he was innocent. The judge sentenced them both to fifteen years of penal servitude.

At 6 a.m. on 2 August, Michael Gilligan was taken from his cell in Durham Gaol to expiate for the crime for which he had been convicted. He shared the scaffold with two others: William McHugh, aged thirty-six, who was convicted of the murder of Thomas Mooney at Barnard Castle by pushing him over a wall into the River Tees; and Elizabeth Pearson, aged twenty-eight, for murdering her uncle by poisoning with 'strychnine and a mix of iron and cyanide' at Gainford. Mooney and Pearson remained calm, but Gilligan did not and his face was deathly pale as he stepped up to the gallows. The executioner was William Marwood and the three were hanged together, dying instantly.

Was the case against Gilligan proved 'beyond reasonable doubt'? No less than three witnesses said they saw him strike the fatal blow, but the assault on John Kilcran took place in darkness, on ill-lit streets. Did the three witnesses who swore it was him have a clear enough view to be certain? One wonders about their accuracy and even honesty; the rival factions of the two Irish groups may have led to a 'tit for tat' response to other, past deeds, including the attack from the previous night.

None of the accused men, of course, were able to defend themselves. This case again highlights the unfairness of the law that stood at that time, namely that accused persons were not permitted to testify. It was not until they had been convicted and they were asked if they had anything to say that Gilligan, Durkin or Flynn were able to speak up, which was too late to be of use to the jury.

Murder so Cruel

Tunstall, 1883

Suspect:	*James Burton*
Age:	33
Charge:	*Murder*
Sentence:	*Execution*

At 8.05 p.m. on Tuesday, 8 May 1883, John Stephenson, an engine driver, and his stoker, Joseph Coates, drove their colliery train through Tunstall along the Ryhope to Silksworth railway. They saw nothing untoward on the journey, but when they returned some twenty minutes later they saw an umbrella lying by the side of the tracks at Silksworth cutting, and when they went to investigate they found the body of a woman. They saw that the woman was 'quite dead'. She was lying face down with her arms under her body, with three stones lying on her head, two more on her back and others on her hips and legs. The railwaymen thought she must have fallen down the steep embankment and the stones had been disturbed and tumbled down after her, half burying her.

Stephenson and Coates reported what they had discovered, and drill instructor Thomas Archer went to the scene with volunteers and removed the body to the Lord Seaham Inn, Silksworth. Sergeant Kendrew of the Durham County force attended the scene, and saw there was a hole in the gutter by the railway tracks that contained blood as well as a 'good many' footprints about the embankment. Isabella Scott, a domestic servant employed by Mr Brews, a solicitor of St George's Square in Sunderland, identified the dead woman as

Elizabeth Ann Burton, aged seventeen, who had worked at the same place. She was the daughter of Joseph Sharp, a screenman at a local colliery.

Dr Lane examined the body at the inn and saw a number of wounds to the head, body and legs. When he conducted the post-mortem examination, he found extensive injuries to the 'brain substance' corresponding with a wound on top of the head, and there was a fracture to the base of the skull, which he pronounced as the cause of death. These injuries, he said, were the result of Elizabeth being struck repeatedly from behind by a blunt instrument, causing her to fall to her knees, after which she had received the blow to the back of the head and the top of the skull. He was unable to say what the instrument might have been, but was able to say that she had been pregnant when she died.

Elizabeth was married to seagoing fireman James Burton, aged thirty-three, of Henry Street, Sunderland. James Burton belonged to a respectable family of Sunderland watermen. His grandfather was master of the first steam tug that plied upon the River Wear and his father was a policeman with the River Wear force. As a child he sustained an injury to his head when he fell from a hayloft, which apparently made him eccentric, morose and of retiring habits. In

Victorian Sunderland. (Reproduced by kind permission of Andrew Clark and George Nairn)

1882, he had sustained an injury to his hand at sea, and so became an inmate of Sunderland infirmary, where he met Elizabeth Sharp, also in hospital suffering from 'some injury'. He had also served several terms of imprisonment with hard labour for offences of violence.

They were married on 10 January 1883, but Elizabeth had since found out that Burton was already married. His wife was Grace Burton, *née* Sidney, and they had had four children, all of whom were dead. Elizabeth refused to go on living with Burton and had returned to service. The police quickly ascertained that Burton had been making threats against Elizabeth, and at 6.30 a.m. on Thursday 10 May, Sergeant Kendrew and Detective Ince, of the Sunderland Borough force, saw him in Avon Street and arrested him for the murder of his 'wife'. When charged, he replied, 'Well, I am clear of that. I have not seen her since Sunday afternoon.'

The police found blood on his clothing and seized them for examination. Burton was also in possession of two bottles labelled 'laudanum, poison', one of which was smeared with blood, and he had a rag wrapped around his left hand which concealed a wound he claimed was an old injury. When he was placed in a cell he borrowed some flannel from another occupant and tried to hang himself with it. His fellow prisoner struggled to take the flannel from him, by which time Burton was 'black in the face'. His life saved, no one could have known that he would have died a better death then than that which awaited him in due course on the gallows.

At noon that same day, Burton appeared before magistrate Major Briggs and some of the evidence was heard. First, from a young blacksmith named Moore, who said he had seen Elizabeth and a man looking like Burton near the scene of the murder on the evening in question. Then a bus driver, who knew Burton well, said that Burton had asked him about the 'residence of the deceased' during the past week, saying she was his wife and no one else should have her. He had made threats about 'what he would do' to any man he caught with her. Detective Ince said Burton had been pointed out to him by two boys as he was running away, and when caught had said, 'I suppose it's me you want.' Throughout proceedings Burton whimpered and wept, and insisted he had not seen his wife since Sunday afternoon.

That same day, the inquest into Elizabeth's death opened at the Lord Seaham Inn and the coroner, Mr May, presided. Evidence was heard from

Elizabeth's father and those who attended the railway cutting where she was found. Dr Lane stated that the wounds were inflicted by a blunt instrument 'using great force', and that she could not have lived 'more than a minute or two' after receiving them. The inquest was adjourned, but opened again the following Monday when more witnesses' testimonies were heard. They included Isabella Scott, who said that Elizabeth had the left the house of her employer shortly after seven o'clock on the Tuesday evening. The clothes she had worn that day were produced – a black dress and grey jacket – which Isabella confirmed were Elizabeth's.

Next to give evidence was locomotive fireman John Wilson who said he had known James Burton about three weeks. He said that Burton had been looking for his wife 'up and down all the streets' and he'd asked her mother, Mrs Sharp, to let him know if she had seen her. On the Tuesday at 10 a.m., Wilson saw Burton in the shipping office and they met up again that afternoon, arranging to 'meet two lasses' at six o'clock beside the fountain in the park. Wilson and Burton went to the south gate of the park, then to the to the north gate, where Burton declared, 'Here's the wife coming, Jack.' Wilson saw a young woman approaching from the direction of Fawcett Street carrying an umbrella and dressed in a black dress with a grey jacket. Burton approached the young woman, shook hands with her and on leaving said to Wilson, 'I am going with my wife to Silksworth to her father's and mother's', and followed the young woman as she walked away quickly.

Constable William Murray said that on 2 May he was on duty in Durham Road, Sunderland when he saw two women and a man, who he identified as James Burton. One of the women (Elizabeth) approached him, and pointing to the man said, 'Officer, this man will persist in following me. I want shot of him.'

'Is he your husband?' asked Murray.

'No,' she replied.

'I am your husband,' said Burton, but the young woman told the policeman she wanted nothing to do with him. The officer told her that if he had not done anything wrong there was nothing he could do. Then Burton said to the woman, 'Lizzie, why won't you live with me? I have never done anything wrong to you.'

'I don't want your half-pay. I can work for myself and my father can work for himself and his family,' she replied.

'I don't drink my money and I don't gamble it,' Burton said.

'You have been married before, and your wife is alive,' she said, before telling PC Murray that her name was Elizabeth Sharp.

The following Tuesday, 8 May – the day of the murder – at about eight o'clock in the evening, Constable Murray was on duty near Ashbrooke Hall, about 300 yards from Tunstall Road, when he saw Burton and Elizabeth, who he said was carrying an umbrella. Burton was walking about four yards behind her and Elizabeth seemed to run when they reached the corner. Alas, the inaction of the policeman enabled James Burton to murder his wife. Not surprisingly, the coroner's jury returned a verdict of 'Wilful Murder'.

The trial of James Burton was heard before Justice Hawkins at the Durham Assizes that July, where he pleaded 'not guilty'. Mr Skidmore, for the prosecution, said that there was no evidence that could justify reducing the crime to manslaughter – it was all or nothing for James Burton.

Joseph Sharp, Elizabeth's father, said that on 10 January that year Burton had married his daughter, and at the time believed him to be an unmarried man. Neither Joseph Sharp nor his wife had given their blessing. He said Elizabeth and Burton had lived together until 24 April when she left him to go into service, and that the last time he saw his daughter alive was on 2 May, when she came to his house with her sister. Burton had followed them and pleaded with Elizabeth to live with him again. She said she would not because of his 'ill-usage' towards her, and accused him of trying to strangle her one night when she was in bed. Burton replied, 'Lizzie, Lizzie, be careful what you are saying'.

'Jim, Jim, you know you did it,' she had replied. He implored her to live with him again, but again she refused.

Elizabeth told her parents she would go to her employer's house, evidently worried about what her employers would say if she did not do so. She and her sister then left, and once again Burton followed them.

Henderson Moor Park, a blacksmith, said he had been standing against the bridge at Tunstall Hope on the Tuesday night at about 8.22 p.m. when he heard a shrill scream. He was able to be precise about the time because he had a train to catch and had checked his watch. He went on to the bridge to see if he could see anything and saw 'two figures coming around the turn'. He thought it was someone 'having a lark' and took no notice other than that they were a man and a woman, and that the woman was carrying an umbrella. They were about twenty yards away and when they reached the bridge the woman jumped over the railings, followed by the man. She ran up the embankment and the man followed, then he raised his hands to take hold of her but failed to do so. The woman reached the top of the embankment and the man followed. Park saw them proceed along the railway for about forty yards before he lost sight of them.

Mr Skidmore summed up the prosecution's case by saying that Elizabeth was in Burton's company when she was last seen alive, and within a short distance of where her body was found moments later. She had been 'foully murdered', and he scorned any attempt to show she had fallen over the embankment or been struck by blocks of limestone falling onto her. Mr Strachan, for the defence, submitted that 'the theory of falling down the embankment' was feasible, and that the case was 'brimful of doubt'. The jury disagreed, taking twenty minutes to find Burton guilty as charged. The judge, now wearing the black cap, said Burton was guilty of 'the murder of a poor young woman to whom you owed every obligation and whom you were bound to protect and shield, a murder so cruel that in common pity and mercy to you I forbear to add to its harrowing tale by any words of mine.' When his Lordship finished speaking, Burton turned and walked 'with a firm step' from the dock.

The execution of James Burton was set for Monday 6 August and he made a full confession to the crime the day before. And thus the scene was set for justice to take its course. Justice of a fashion as it would turn out, for no one deserves the fate that awaited James Burton at the hands of the State at Durham Gaol.

The hangman William Marwood. (Author's collection)

Burton was taken from his cell and pinioned a little before 8 a.m. and it seems he offered slight resistance because William Marwood, the executioner, fastened the strap too tight, prompting Burton to complain three times, to which Marwood replied that if it was too tight it would be all the better for him. On the gallows, Marwood, who had eleven years' experience as a hangman, set his 'victim' under the beam and, after 'a little jerky pushing', got him into position immediately beneath the dangling rope. As the chaplain prayed, and Burton muttered suitable responses, Marwood drew the cap over his face then fastened the rope about his neck, fixing the iron thimble at the carotid artery under the ear. The rope having been adjusted to Marwood's satisfaction, he measured the length of slack that reached down to Burton's hip. All of these preparations would have only taken a short time.

The head warder then noticed that the chaplain was standing slightly on the drop and moved him back. This seems to have affected Marwood who appeared to act hurriedly, and not calmly and methodical as observed on his past 'lamentable visits on similar errands'. As the chaplain uttered the words, 'Oh Lord, receive the soul of this man about to die', Marwood pulled the lever and Burton 'shot with a painful jerk' down into the cavity and disappeared from view. But his ordeal, far from being over, was only just beginning.

Something had gone horribly wrong, for the rope was seen to swing wildly from side to side, and this was followed by a 'strong jerking'. Looking down into the cavity, those present saw that the rope had entangled around the back of Burton's neck and was strung under his armpits and across his chest. Marwood, assisted by another warder, pulled 'its living burden' back up to the edge of the cavity, and Burton's still-pinioned elbows came to rest on the cross-timber, close by the lever. He was speedily placed into a sitting position, by which time his cap had ruffled up to his eyes and his face was 'ghastly pale'. But that he was 'alive and in full possession of his senses' was certain, as he was heard to mutter more than once, 'Oh Lord, save my soul.'

Marwood untangled the rope and adjusted it before seizing Burton by the shoulders and hurling him back through the open doors of the drop. As Burton swung violently right and left, Marwood grabbed the rope to try and steady the movement. There were 'two or three significant jerks' followed by a series of twitches lasting half a minute before the ghastly procedure came to a merciful conclusion and Burton was finally dead. The black flag was raised, signifying to the fifty or so people outside the prison that the sentence had been carried out. They did not know then of its manner, but when 'details of the horrifying incident' were released there was 'considerable excitement' in the city.

James Burton paid the ultimate price of his brutal crime, perpetrated upon a young girl whose only wish was to be rid of him. Had Constable William Murray not ignored Elizabeth Sharp's complaints on two occasions, or

A depiction of the botched execution of James Burton. (Author's collection)

Henderson Moor Park raised the alarm when he heard her screams and saw her being pursued, they might have been able to save her. As for Burton, he paid the penalty of murdering Elizabeth Sharp in the most harrowing of circumstances.

Marwood was called by the coroner to attend the inquest into Burton's death (as required by law) and questioned about what had happened at the execution. He was even told to go and fetch the rope, which he did. After interrogation by both the coroner and the foreman of the jury, Marwood bid the jurymen 'good morning' and departed. 'It all seems to have been accidental,' said the foreman. 'We have nothing to do with that,' declared the coroner, who then closed proceedings.

'The Poor Polis'

Butterknowle, 1884

Suspects:	*Wlliam Siddle, Joseph Hodgson and Joseph Lowson*
Ages:	*23, 20, 25*
Charges:	*Murder*
Sentences:	*Execution*

Until a generation ago it was normal practice for policemen to patrol on foot, alone, without recourse to immediate assistance. As such they showed a presence to the public as well as enforcing the law, a role demanding initiative and courage. The role of the 'polis' was especially dangerous at weekends, when young pit lads were enjoying a well-earned pint in a local hostelry. So it was on the night of Saturday, 23 February 1884, when Acting Sergeant William Smith stepped from his house to go on patrol in Butterknowle. It was a dark, rainy night, but Smith had a job to do and he set off alone to show the presence of the law.

Just before ten o'clock, Smith was outside the Royal Oak Inn at the west end of the village, where he chanced upon Robert Lamb. The two men walked together as far as Lamb's house at the far end of the village, and on the way they passed the Diamond Inn. The pub had been busy that night, patronised by fifty or so men who had earlier attended a pigeon shoot nearby. Those in attendance included miners William Siddle, aged twenty-three, Joseph Hodgson, aged twenty, and Joseph Lowson, aged twenty five. They left along with the rest of the customers at ten o'clock, the pub's closing time.

Acting Sergeant Smith and Lamb were passing as the pub 'turned out'. One or more of the group 'snittered' at the policeman. In any event, Smith and Lamb continued on their way. Smith left Lamb at his house, saying he was going on to The Slack – a small hamlet about half a mile away down Diamond Hill. Meanwhile, William Siddle turned up at the house of Benjamin Smedley, along with a man called Grey, who requested a light for his pipe. Joseph Lowson's face also appeared at the door and there was another unidentified man lurking outside. They all walked off along the road.

One can imagine the scene that night as the men made their way home after drinking for five hours. Some made their way home in groups and others left on their own; a few lived nearby, whilst others lived further afield, with the varying journeys a mixture of having to walk the dark roads or across the fields. Tailor William Akeman had not been drinking that night and left home to walk to Butterknowle, passing three groups of men on the

The Diamond Inn, Butterknowle. (© Paul Heslop)

road. He recognised men in the first two groups but none in the third, who spoke in whispers as he approached on Diamond Hill. One of them brushed drunkenly against him as they passed. As Akeman continued on his way, he encountered Acting Sergeant Smith as the officer was making his way down Diamond Hill to The Slack.

Soon afterwards, two doctors were making their way up Diamond Hill, having just left The Slack. As men of the medical profession John Jamieson Middleton and his assistant, Gordon Bowker Gorrick, were supposed to be upstanding citizens and their credibility would be expected to stand up well to public scrutiny; however, on that night they were just as drunk as the men who had recently left the Diamond Inn.

As they walked up the hill, Middleton stopped at the old Diamond Pit engine house, possibly to relieve himself. Forty yards further on, Gorrick, continuing towards the village, saw a man standing by the side of the road. The man spoke to Gorrick, saying, 'The poor polis.' When Gorrick asked him what the matter was the man pointed up the hill. A little way up the road, Gorrick found Acting Sergeant Smith lying on the ground, his head in the gutter. The policeman was breathing heavily, but his skull had been fractured and Gorrick knew he was dying. When the doctor looked around for the man he was no longer there.

Continuing up the hill, Middleton spotted Gorrick and the prostrate form of Acting Sergeant Smith. Even as they attended the victim, the doctors were attacked by three men, who ran from the direction of the engine house throwing stones at them. They saw the men were all of different height, Middleton ran up the hill, shouting 'Murder!' and 'Help!' As their assailants fled into the darkness other men appeared and the doctors again turned their attention to Smith. As well as a fractured skull, other injuries consisted of a series of contused wounds and several of Smith's teeth had been knocked out. His hands were lacerated, either through his endeavours to protect himself or from falling. Middleton concluded that the injuries were caused by being kicked or by someone throwing stones. Smith died at the scene and was removed to his home.

The first policeman on the scene was Constable George Knight of Cockfield, who examined the spot where Middleton and Gorrick had found his colleague. He found bricks and stones, which had been almost certainly thrown at Smith as he walked down Diamond Hill. At Smith's house he

Site of the former engine house on Diamond Hill, Butterknowle.
(© Paul Heslop)

examined his coat – covered in blood and dirt – and found Smith's truncheon in the pocket, which was apparently unused. Sergeant Patrick Daley later examined the scene with his lamp, finding a pearl button lying close to some blood and a large, flat stone stained with blood.

About five o'clock the following morning, Daley went to a house at Lands, about a mile away, accompanied by other officers, where they found William Siddle sharing a bed with Joseph Hodgson (a common practice then). Hodgson said he had been to 'Simpson's', meaning the Diamond Inn in Butterknowle, leaving the premises at ten o'clock with Joseph Lowson. They walked down Diamond Hill and over Bowes Hill, where Siddle overtook them. He had not quarrelled with anyone. Siddle said he too had been at Simpson's, leaving at ten o'clock. He agreed he had overtaken Hodgson and Lowson on Bowes Hill, and they all walked home together then, he said.

Daley took possession of Siddle's trousers, coat and waistcoat, and a coat and a pair of shoes belonging to Hodgson. Then he handcuffed them and went to Lowson's house, who said he too had been at Simpson's, leaving at closing time, and that he had walked home with Hodgson and met Siddle on the road. Asked what clothes he had worn he pointed to a coat and trousers hanging by the fire, which were wet and recently washed. Daley took possession of them, his boots and his shirt, from which a button was missing – the shirt buttons matched the one found at the scene of the crime. All three men were taken to Staindrop police station and charged with the murder of Acting Sergeant Smith.

Acting Sergeant Smith was murdered in the most brutal circumstances. Thirty-nine years old and married with seven children, he had spent his sixteen years' service in the Barnard Castle division and lived in the police house at Lynesack, a mile from Butterknowle. It is difficult to find a motive for the crime other than the consumption of alcohol. It was thought that having stoned and beaten him to death, the perpetrators clambered onto a nearby pit heap, one of them remaining on Diamond Hill to inform Dr Gorrick of the 'poor polis' before they had all fled.

The murdered policeman was buried in the peaceful cemetery of the Church of St John the Evangelist in Lynesack. The funeral procession included eighty-two police officers and was headed by the Woodlands Band playing the Dead March – a scene described as having 'no parallel' in the county of Durham. Also in the procession were Smith's wife and children, and his aged father. In this quiet backwater of County Durham – the scene is largely unchanged today, save for the removal of the scars of industry – it must have been quite a sight. A relief fund for the murdered officer's family raised monies from nearby collieries and pitmen alike. There was, alas, no pension for the bereaved in those days.

With no admissions from suspects and identification being unsatisfactory, the police would have to rely on whatever other evidence they could muster to prove their case. There was the pearl button found at the scene, and Lowson's recently-washed garments, which may have been stained with blood prior to laundering. But it was difficult, if not impossible, in those days to even establish whether blood was human let alone that of a particular individual. At the inquest into Acting Sergeant Smith's death, held at the Royal Oak Inn, Butterknowle before coroner Thomas Dean, County Analyst William Stock gave evidence of his examination of the bloodstained clothing and could only state that the blood 'must have been either human or the blood of an animal'.

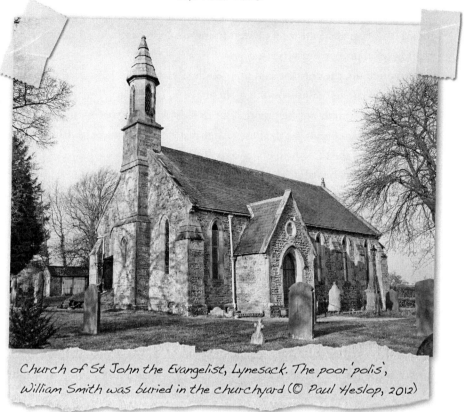

Church of St John the Evangelist, Lynesack. The poor 'polis',
William Smith was buried in the churchyard (© Paul Heslop, 2012)

Annie Hooper, Sergeant Daley's sister-in-law, said that on Sunday
24 February she was staying at the police house at Staindrop as a guest, and
at about 7.15 that evening she was in the passage close to the cells when
she overheard Lowson say, 'They cannot prove nowt against us, they only
have us on suspicion. Dinnat thou tell them nowt Bill. Just say thou went
straight home.' Siddle replied to this, saying, 'Thou knows it's reet.' This
'evidence' would not be admissible today.

Three men had been seen heading in the direction of Lands by William
Akeman and were of 'irregular height', as were the suspects. With this in
mind, Akeman attended Barnard Castle police station where he saw a line of
men and picked out Siddle, and said the tallest (Lowson) 'corresponded' in
height and build to one of the men he saw near the engine house. At Staindrop
police station he was shown four men, one of whom 'corresponded' in height
with the middle-sized man of the three (Hodgson). Using just height and

build is not an accurate way of identifying suspects, and would not play any part in legal proceedings today.

Summing up, the coroner said that Siddle, Lowson and Hodgson 'were seen together in the neighbourhood on the night in question'. The evidence was only circumstantial, but he pointed out that evidence of that nature had been 'held by some judges to be the best'. After just twenty minutes of deliberation, the jury found the three men guilty of wilful murder.

The case was heard at the Durham Assizes before Justice Hawkins that May and all three men pleaded 'not guilty' to the murder of Acting Sergeant Smith. For the prosecution, Mr Skidmore told the jury that if they found one of the prisoners had committed the murder and that the others were privy to it, then they too would be guilty.

John Lawson Putter said that on the night in question he was at Simpson's and on leaving at about ten o'clock he saw Acting Sergeant Smith standing outside. He said that as they left the pub, the prisoners 'snittered' at the police officer to express their dislike of him. The group of men walked down the road and as they reached the bend, Siddle said, 'Let's go back and rib the polis.' Putter said Siddle and Hodgson went back 'twenty or thirty yards' but came back again. A man named Moore said, 'Don't thou go back, Josh, thou gan yam [home]'. Hodgson and Lowson left the group, and Siddle did the same, saying he would 'seek his mates'.

William Akeman gave evidence of 'identification', saying the accused were in the third group of men he saw on the road near to the scene of the crime. This identification can hardly be relied upon, as proximity hardly proves they murdered the policeman.

Dr Middleton and Dr Gorrick had little chance to identify Smith's assailants. They did not witness the attack and could not identify the

The Royal Oak, Butterknowle: scene of the inquest into the death of Acting Sergeant Smith. (© Paul Heslop)

men who threw stones at them afterwards. Even so, one might have expected better from two professional men when it came to giving evidence at a murder trial.

Gorrick said he had been at The Slack when, at 'about sixteen minutes past ten o'clock', he and Dr Middleton were proceeding up Diamond Hill when he encountered a man who said, 'The poor polis.' He saw three men, ten or fifteen yards away, whom he said 'resembled' the prisoners. Under cross-examination he said he had been at Bishop Auckland with Dr Middleton and the two of them had visited three public houses. They travelled by the last train to Cockfield, visiting the Stag's Head. Although he said, 'I was not drunk', he did admit to falling over at Cockfield Station. 'Dr Middleton was as sober as I was,' he said, to laughter in court.

Dr Middleton said he had examined Smith and found that he had a fractured skull, which was the cause of death. Blows with a foot or stones would have caused the injuries. He saw three men appear from the old engine sheds and throw stones, but couldn't say he recognised them in court.

Diamond Hill today. The stone wall where Acting Sergeant Smith met his fate is on the right. (© Paul Heslop)

Middleton did not answer questions 'readily', and the judge told him to take his hands out of his pockets and pay attention. 'Rouse yourself up,' said his Lordship, 'or if you would like to have a nap have one. The questions are intelligible enough.' Middleton was pressed about how much he had to drink, and where.

'I had a glass of beer. I also had a glass of whisky.' There was more laughter in court and his Lordship responded, 'If there is any more unseemly laughter I will order the public gallery to be cleared. There are three men being tried for murder. This is not a playhouse.' After Middleton stumbled through more questions, which Middleton seemed unable to answer, the judge told him to do justice to himself as a professional man, but the doctor had little more of value to impart.

Sergeant Daley said he had found a pearl button at the scene and that it corresponded with the buttons on Lowson's shirt, but he then discredited himself by declaring Doctors Middleton and Gorrick to be sober on the night. William Stock was next to give evidence, and he reiterated the results of his examination of the bloodstained coat.

Mr Lockwood, for the defence, at once attacked the testimony of Doctors Middleton and Gorrick, saying neither of the pair was in the state to be able to identify the prisoners with accuracy. The shirt button, he said, was 'of an ordinary kind' and there were a dozen men at the scene of the murder that could have lost a button.

Mr Lockwood called upon his witnesses. Thomas Thompson, a surveyor, said that none of the coke ovens in the neighbourhood threw any light on the road at the scene of the murder, reducing even further the chances of identification. Several witnesses from licensed premises and elsewhere said both doctors were intoxicated. Annie Parker, of the Stag's Head, said they were drunk when they arrived and were even boxing one another. Elizabeth Simpson, of Lands, said about a fortnight before she was at Lowson's house when his young daughter fell and cut her lip. Lowson took her upon his knee and blood spilled on to the floor, although she did not actually see any spill on to his clothes it was a possible explanation for blood being on the garment.

The jury returned guilty verdicts against Lowson and Siddle, but found Hodgson not guilty and he was released. It is difficult, if not impossible, to understand the logic in this decision: one might think any one of the accused men was guilty, or all or none of them, since no hard evidence was forthcoming against any individual.

Asked if they had anything to say before sentence, both Lowson and Siddle denied the crime and had more to say besides. After a harrowing exchange the judge assumed the black cap and sentenced them to death. Both men responded with more denials, Siddle resorting to profanities. They were removed from the dock even as Lowson was calling out, 'I am an innocent man. There has been nothing but perjury said against me.' Hodgson, meanwhile, 'seemed dazed at his escape from the jaws of death' and could barely speak.

Languishing in prison, Siddle wrote to his parents swearing his innocence. 'It hurts me to think that I should be hanged for a thing that I am clear of.' Meanwhile, people in south-west Durham had doubts about the convictions and a thousand men attended a meeting at Willington, where speakers addressed the crowd. A resolution was passed that, 'In the opinion of the householders of Willington and district the evidence was of a very weak and contradictory nature and allowed considerable cause for doubt ... This meeting is of the opinion that a resolution should be forwarded to the Home Secretary praying for the remission of the sentences or a reinvestigation of the case'. Another meeting held at Evenwood followed, where they too disagreed with the outcome of the trial, advocating a reprieve.

There followed a dramatic turn of events when Lowson made two statements – one confessing to the crime and declaring Siddle to be innocent, the other affirming that he (Lowson) and 'another man, not in custody', were the guilty parties. These statements were laid before the Home Secretary who sent a commissioner to Durham to examine this new evidence in private. The result was a reprieve for Siddle, leaving Lowson alone to face the consequences.

Joseph Lowson was hanged by James Berry on the 'bright May morning' of Tuesday, 27 May 1884. In an interview with the press, Berry said Lowson cursed both the chaplain and executioner, of whom he enquired, 'Who the hell are you?' Berry reported that Lowson declared, 'I might as well tell you that Hodgson struck the first blow. I struck the second. We did the job betwixt us. Siddle is an innocent man.' Berry also said Lowson was the bravest man he had ever hanged. Hodgson, of course, having been charged and acquitted could not

This arrow, chiselled into a stone in the wall on Diamond Hill, marks the site of the murder of Acting Sergeant Smith. (© Paul Heslop)

then be retried. Even if he could, such a course of action would have ended with another acquittal, since one of the main witnesses was now deceased.

Today, an arrow chiselled into a stone wall on Diamond Hill marks the spot where William Smith met his death; a crude and poignant reminder of the grim events in the village of Butterknowle that night.

'Unhinged in his Mind'

Durham City, 1888

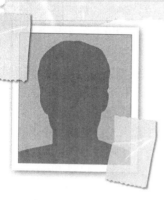

Suspect: Benjamin Wright

Age: 43

Charge: Murder

Sentence: Suspect committed
            suicide to escape justice

On the last day of every month every divisional superintendent in the Durham County police force would travel to Durham City to collect the wages for the officers under his command; Thursday, 31 May 1888 was no different. Superintendent Joseph Scott, in charge of the Jarrow Division, would travel by train to Durham. This particular time he was escorting a prisoner, John Fannen, a Hebburn miner, who had been unable to pay a fine imposed by the magistrates and had been committed to custody in Durham Gaol. Standing over 6ft tall, with twenty-four years' service and described as a man of 'remarkable physique', Scott had no problem escorting his prisoner alone.

On that fateful morning, the pair travelled from South Shields to Newcastle then on to Durham, where on arrival Scott and Fannen began their walk to the prison. From the railway station they walked down the North Road towards the river and crossed Framwellgate Bridge, only a ten-minute walk from the prison gate. Across the bridge, the road led up to the narrow confines of Silver Street, a busy thoroughfare then as it is today.

As the two men walked side by side in the middle of the road, a third man approached them from behind. He was carrying a rifle, which he pointed directly at the superintendent's back. When the man was immediately behind the superintendent and his charge, he pulled the trigger and shot the superintendent at point-blank range. As Superintendent Scott fell, mortally wounded, the man threw the rifle to the ground and, after fumbling in his coat pocket, produced a revolver and shot himself in the head.

The two injured men lay where they fell for about ten minutes 'in the centre of a horrified crowd' – that included Scott's prisoner, John Fannen, who made no attempt to escape – until the arrival of Superintendent Smith of the city force. Smith had Superintendent Scott taken to the nearby Red Lion public house, where he later died, and his assassin to Castle Hotel where he too died ten minutes later. He was quickly identified as Benjamin Wright, a former sergeant in the county force who had served under Scott at Hebburn, and who had been dismissed from the force nine months before.

Joseph Scott was aged forty-four, and one of two brothers who had attained the rank of superintendent in the Durham County force. He joined the force in 1863 at just twenty years of age, and served as inspector at Darlington for ten years, before being promoted and transferred to Jarrow. Until a few months before he shot Superintendent Scott, ex-Sergeant Wright had served

Framwellgate Bridge and River Wear, Durham. (© Paul Heslop)

under him at Hebburn, in the Jarrow division, but the previous August, 'in consequence of serious irregularities', Wright had been reduced in rank to Constable and transferred to Darlington, where he was dismissed from the force. After that, reported the *Durham County Advertiser*, Wright became 'unhinged in his mind'. He lived at Merrington (now Kirk Merrington) with his wife and family, but travelled frequently to Durham with a view to being reinstated in the force. Only the previous Tuesday he had visited the County Police Barracks requesting to see the chief constable, but an inspector, 'noticing his wild and excited manner', and seeing that he had something in his coat pocket, 'prudently refused to conduct him to the chief constable's office'. The object turned out to be a revolver.

The inquest into the deaths of Scott and Wright were held in Durham City police station within three hours of the tragic events of that day. The coroner was Mr C. Maynard. The 'horrible and blood-besmeared bodies' were first viewed by the jury.

Several witnesses were able to describe the events in Silver Street. Prisoner John Fannen said the first he knew of anything untoward was the sound of a gunshot, and on turning around he saw Wright throw the rifle to the ground before shooting himself with a revolver, which he had taken from his coat pocket. Superintendent Scott, he said, groaned and fell to the ground. He did not hear Wright utter a word and did not see where he came from.

(© Paul Heslop)

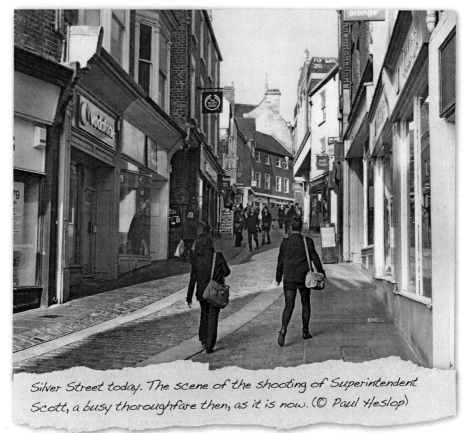

Silver Street today. The scene of the shooting of Superintendent Scott, a busy thoroughfare then, as it is now. (© Paul Heslop)

John Henry Thorn, a fruiterer, was standing behind the counter of his shop in Silver Street, and saw Scott and Fannen outside. He then saw Wright, who was just outside the shop door, approach Scott from behind and shoot him in the back at close range. Thorn ran into the street just in time to see Wright shoot himself in the head. Honor Thougood, of the nearby Red Lion, was standing in the bar when she saw Wright 'take three quick steps behind Scott and fire the gun at his back'. She looked away and did not see Wright shoot himself.

Dr Alfred Mason Vann happened to be in Silver Street at about 10.45 that morning when he saw a crowd, and as he passed the Red Lion Superintendent Smith saw him and called him inside. There, in the passage, he saw the body of Superintendent Scott. He then went across to the Castle Hotel yard where he saw Wright lying in one of the stables. Wright was alive and bleeding from the mouth. Vann examined him and found a wound on the left side of the roof of the throat, there was also swelling on the left temple where the bone seemed to be broken. Wright was given brandy and water but died soon afterwards.

Vann described Scott's injuries as a round wound close to the spine at the seventh rib and another more ragged wound in the chest. Shot at such close range the bullet had passed into and out of Scott's body, in a slanting direction through the lungs. Superintendent Smith said the gun Wright had used to shoot himself was a German-made six-chamber revolver and that five bullets remained in the weapon. The coroner asked the superintendent if he knew what Wright 'had been doing' since he had been dismissed from the force. Smith said he did not think he had been doing anything. 'He must have been a labourer, then,' said the coroner. Unsurprisingly, the jury's verdict was that Benjamin Wright had 'feloniously, wilfully and of malice aforethought murdered Superintendent Joseph Scott'.

The coroner then opened the inquest into the death of Benjamin Wright. Inspector Thomas Wilkinson said that Wright was forty-three years of age and had been dismissed from the force on 13 August for disobedience of

A national icon, Durham Cathedral. (© Paul Heslop)

orders. The coroner asked him if he knew if Wright had had any ill-will against anyone. 'I saw him on Tuesday last,' replied Wilkinson, 'and from his appearance I did not consider him to be a sane man. He talked very incoherently. I asked him some questions but he could not give me a proper answer.' He had a grievance, said Wilkinson, but would not tell anyone what it was. He had seen him four times since his dismissal and on each occasion he had looked wilder than before. 'He looked as if he was gradually going wrong,' he said, adding that Wright had been trying to get back into the force.

Wright's movements leading up to the tragic events in Silver Street were recounted by several witnesses. The first, Constable Fryer, stationed at Sunderland Bridge (between Kirk Merrington and Durham), said he was on his way to Durham that morning, around twenty minutes to nine, when about a mile on the Durham side of Sunderland Bridge he saw Wright approximately twenty or thirty yards in front of him. Wright went to a water trough and started to wash his hands. PC Fryer said 'Good morning,' but Wright ignored him. 'Is that you?' asked the officer, but Wright only mumbled a reply. Fryer had noticed Wright was carrying something under his arm, which he had set down by the wall, putting his leg against it as he washed his hands. Fryer did not linger. 'I hadn't time,' he said.

Jane Cowley of the Neville Hotel in Durham did not know Wright, but identified him by looking at his body and confirmed that he was the same man who came into the hotel about ten o'clock that morning and had a glass of whisky. He had sat in the bay window in the Commercial Room facing the road, with a view of people leaving the railway station. He was there for about three-quarters of an hour. She did not enquire of his business and remarked only on the weather being 'blowy' that morning, to which Wright replied 'Yes, it is.' She did not see if he was carrying anything.

John Hull, a groom, said he saw Superintendent Scott bringing a prisoner down the North Road and Wright walking immediately behind carrying 'something like a gun' in a cover. At Framwellgate Bridge he noticed that Wright was still walking behind the two men. When Hull got to the Castle Hotel he heard a shot, then another. He saw the men lying on the ground and said Superintendent Scott 'never stirred', whilst Wright's 'eyes and mouth were going as if he was choking with blood'.

Inspector Snowdon of Jarrow said he had known Benjamin Wright for some years and had last seen him the previous August. The coroner asked him whether he knew if Superintendent Scott had any reason to fear Wright. 'None whatever,' said Snowdon. He had never intimated any fear? 'Never,' replied Snowdon and added that Wright had never threatened Scott as far as he was aware. He went on to say, 'About the later part of last June, July and August there were three explosions at two private houses and at the police station at Hebburn. Superintendent Scott and I investigated them. Superintendent Scott gave me authority to search Wright's house and I did so. His behaviour was more like that of a lunatic than anything else.'

The coroner then asked, 'What did he do or say?'

Snowdon replied, 'He said it was not him who had caused the explosions, but other people. His manner both in the house and outside was dreadful. He asked the superintendent what the [expletive unknown] made him think it was him who caused the explosions? The superintendent said he had his reasons. He then called the superintendent a [expletive unknown] and said there were no reasons at all. Wright called me the same name. I thought his conduct more like a madman than anything else.'

'What kind of explosions were they?'

'Well, they were each as a man out of his mind was likely to cause, by putting a bottle of gunpowder onto the window sill and firing it. He was not altogether in his mind or for his actions, and was suffering very much from the effects of drink.'

'Was he dismissed in consequence of that?' asked the coroner.

'He was reduced from sergeant to constable and removed to Darlington for intemperance,' Snowdon replied. 'At Darlington we found he had destroyed some books and there were defalcations in the accounts.' Benjamin Wright had been gradually changing for some time, he said. Inspector Harrison of Jarrow said he had known Wright for some years and found him strange in manner, that he was forgetful, mumbling to himself and conducting himself in an indifferent manner in his duties.

'He was unhinged in his mind, and I reported that to Superintendent Scott,' said Harrison.

The coroner then asked, 'Did he ever threaten to injure anybody?'

Harrison replied, 'He always carried a revolver about with him.'

A juror then queried, 'Had he any cause to carry this revolver?'

To which Harrison said, 'No. Not the least.'

The coroner then told the jury it would be for them to decide whether there was sufficient evidence to justify saying Wright was temporarily deranged 'at the time he committed the act' of killing Scott or himself. The jury's verdict was that that Benjamin Wright had committed suicide whilst in an unsound state of mind.

On the day following the shootings, a letter was found on the mantelpiece of Wright's home at Kirk Merrington. The letter was ungrammatical and was contained in an unaddressed envelope, and was written in Wright's handwriting. It read:

> The only good this will do is to be hoped will stimulate superintendents to always speak the truth, and not to resort to scientific lies when giving evidence against brother officers. It would also be better if chief constables would not repose so much confidence in superintendents, for they know this and greatly depend it.

Although the wording is vague, its meaning seems clear enough: that Wright had a grudge against Superintendent Joseph Scott and held the chief constable responsible for demoting him to the lesser rank. It would be their fault that he found himself working in the drudgery of the coke ovens at Leasingthorne where he had found employment, contrary to the belief of his former colleagues (and where he was reproached for negligence in his work). It might be noted here that the speediness of the inquests, just three hours after the deaths of two men, was surely wrong, for the letter had not yet been discovered and its contents should have been of material importance to the jury's considerations. Better to have all available facts, surely, than a swift and unnecessary dispensation of proceedings.

Writing to the *Durham County Advertiser* on 8 June, a correspondent said he had known both men. He described Scott as having a sense of duty and Wright as being negligent and strange, and describing the motive for the killing as one of revenge for imaginary grievances. Yet, said the writer, Scott had regarded Wright as his friend and spoke of him out of pity rather than resentment, regarding him as a 'poor, misguided individual who had become

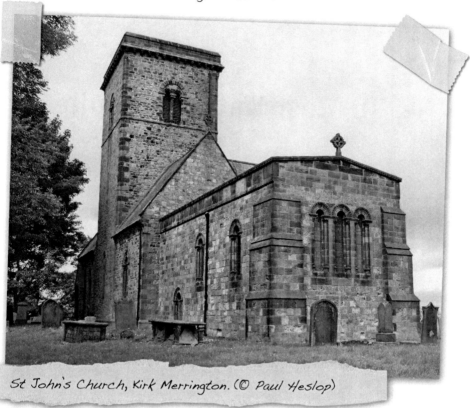

St John's Church, Kirk Merrington. (© Paul Heslop)

deranged with drink'. The correspondent was of the opinion that Wright might do someone an injury, but thought it more probable that he would commit suicide. He or she was right to that extent, at least.

Joseph Scott, cruelly murdered whilst carrying out his duties, was interred in Jarrow Cemetery following a service at St Paul's Church. Benjamin Wright was buried in Kirk Merrington churchyard. It was reported that eighty people attended Wright's funeral, amongst them 'a fair sprinkling of females'.

'In Most Malignant Spite'

Birtley, 1888

Suspect: William Waddle

Age: 22

Charge: Murder

Sentence: Execution

The landscape of County Durham has changed over the years. Today, the area to the north of Birtley, previously known as Birtley North Side, is a maze of roads and roundabouts around Junction 65 of the A1(M) motorway, but it was once a waggonway linking the pits at Ouston and elsewhere with the Tyne, elevated above a footway with a gutter or ditch of varying depths alongside. It was quiet then, a bleak fellside occupied by scattered cottages where miners' families lived before the luxuries of television and motor cars.

At about seven o'clock on the morning of Sunday, 23 September 1888, boilersmith John Fish was walking alongside the waggonway on his way to Ouston Colliery to repair an engine. Whatever thoughts were passing through Fish's mind on that quiet Sunday morning, they would have been harshly interrupted when he saw the body of a young woman lying in the ditch. She lay on her left side, her hands held upward towards her face, possibly in a defensive gesture. She was soaked in blood and no wonder, for her face had been slashed and she had been stabbed repeatedly in the abdomen.

Fish went at once for the local constable, PC Dodds, who went directly to the scene. Dodds saw that the woman had been dead for some hours and she was quickly identified as Jane Beardmore, aged twenty-seven, who lived with her mother and stepfather three-quarters of a mile away in a cottage at Birtley North Side, near to the present-day motorway. Dodds had the body 'removed at once' to her home, where it was established that what little money she had was still in the pocket of her dress, together with some sweets. There was little doubt that her injuries had been inflicted where she was found.

A post-mortem examination was carried out at eight o'clock that morning by Dr Walter Galloway, in the front room of Jane's house. Dr Galloway had much to report; the main injuries comprised a gaping puncture wound on the left side of the face, extending downwards and backwards to the vertebrae. It had been inflicted with a sharp instrument, probably a knife, beginning at the ear and thrusting downwards in a sweeping blow. The wounds to her abdomen were inflicted when she was on the ground and were so severe that some of the small intestines protruded. Dr Galloway recorded these as the cause of death.

The inquest into Jane's death opened on Monday morning at the Three Tuns Hotel in Birtley, which was then a wayside inn. The jury was comprised of 'eighteen good men' and their first task was to view the body, so they made their way across desolate country to a 'low, brick house, well away from the nearest habitation'. Jane had lived with her stepfather, Joseph Savage, her mother, Isabella, and William, her half-brother. Her body lay in the large, downstairs room and must have been a harrowing sight.

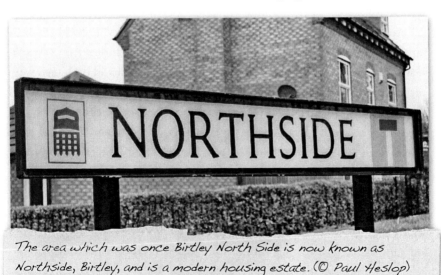

The area which was once Birtley North Side is now known as Northside, Birtley, and is a modern housing estate. (© Paul Heslop)

The jury then went to the scene of the crime, though there was little to see apart from the footmarks of sightseers in the sodden grass. PC Dodds had passed the spot at half past ten the previous evening and not seen anything untoward. But it was dark and he had passed a dozen yards away from where Jane had been found on the opposite side of the waggonway; there was no way of knowing if she had been there at that time.

Jane Beardmore, or Savage, was a single woman. Her mother said that on the Saturday evening at around seven, Jane had gone out, saying she was going to Dolly's – a Mrs Newall's – at North Side Farm, in Birtley. It was the last time she would see her daughter alive. She added that she had 'kept company' with a local man called William Waddle, who had twice been to their house.

That same evening, Jane called at a small inn at Birtley North Side that doubled up as a sweetshop, where she was served by Elizabeth Morris who sold her a penn'orth of toffee. Also present was Isabella McInnes who worked in the shop. A couple of days before, Isabella had 'chaffed' Jane about her keeping company with William Waddle, but Jane told her she no longer was. Jane then went to Birtley North Side Farm, where she was greeted by Mrs Newall. A few minutes later William Waddle came in and sat down. He declined a piece of Jane's toffee and sat sulkily with his head down. Shortly afterwards, Jane went to the door and bade Mrs Newall goodnight. Waddle followed, saying nothing.

Later that evening, Newark Forster, a joiner, was driving a cart-load of furniture on the Black Road from the Vale Pit, near Eighton banks towards North Side Farm. He was accompanied by Henry Brown and both men were sitting on the nearside of the cart. They had crossed the waggonway when they noticed a woman walking in their direction towards the Vale Pit, and when they overtook her she was right alongside the nearside of the cart. The woman was Jane Beardmore, whom Forster knew. The cart being laden with furniture, neither man could see if anyone was walking on the opposite side of it. They saw no other person, only Jane.

The police had two lines of enquiry – the first was regarding William Waddle, a twenty-two-year-old labourer at Birtley Ironworks, who lived in lodgings with widowed Jane McCormack at The Brickgarth. Waddle had not been seen at his lodgings since the Friday evening and did not turn up for work

The Three Tuns at Birtley today. Scene of the inquest into the murder of Jane Beardmore. (© Paul Heslop)

on Monday morning. The police circulated a notice to say that he was wanted in connection with the murder, giving his name and describing him as having 'tender feet and walking with his toes out'.

Waddle's landlady, Mrs McCormack, gave an account of his behaviour on the Saturday, which seemed to lend much weight to the likelihood that he was Jane's killer. She said he came home from work at one o'clock that afternoon, went out again for his wages and returned after four when he was 'very drunk'. He paid for his board and lodgings, and whilst in the house he vomited before going out at seven o'clock to Birtley North Side Farm. Mrs McCormack pleaded with him not to go, but he left the house without speaking and never returned. He never intimated that he would not be coming back. Mrs McCormick did not know whether he had a knife at that or any other time.

The second line of enquiry was quite sensational. Jane's murder happened during the same period that a number of prostitutes were murdered in London and, perhaps significantly, in similar circumstances with their bodies being mutilated and disembowelled – the Jack the Ripper murders at Whitechapel. Post-mortem examinations had shown specific body parts had been removed, leading pathologists to believe the murderer possessed a degree of anatomical knowledge. Because of the similarities between Jane's body and the victims in Whitechapel, Inspector Roots of Scotland Yard and Dr Phillips who had examined the bodies of the London victims, travelled to the North East. Dr Phillips quickly discounted any link between the murders in London and that of Jane, saying they had been 'enacted by a different person'. In the Whitechapel atrocities, disembowelling had been deliberate and extensive; in Jane's case perhaps not so. Inspector Roots said that, in his opinion, Jane's murder was a 'clumsy imitation' of the work of Jack the Ripper. That left the Durham police with the task of finding William Waddle.

The police had a theory: that William Waddle had 'destroyed himself' by throwing himself down one of the many disused mineshafts in the locality. Some were very deep and had not been penetrated for years, so it was possible he might never be found. Meanwhile, following the widespread publicity the 'sightings' of the suspect were manifold: a man of Waddle's description was reportedly seen at a coke oven at Byers Green near Spennymoor; someone else was sure they had seen him in Westgate Hill in Newcastle; there was a rumour that he had been captured near Heaton railway station when a crowd followed a policeman who had arrested a man, only to find he was unconnected with the murder at Birtley; he was sighted at Seaham Harbour asking for directions to Hartlepool; Police Constable Minto found a pair of old boots near Annfield Plain, where it was asserted that Waddle had once been employed at the Lizzie Colliery; a suspicious man had been seen loitering in Consett; at Ouston a strange man presented himself at someone's door asking for bread, but when asked to wait he disappeared, and bloodstained clothing was found at Lamesley – a possible escape route for the murderer to take – but there was no firm trace on William Waddle.

They buried Jane Beardmore in the parish churchyard at Birtley. At the graveside the Reverend Watts said, 'A terrible deed has been done ... doubtless begun in anger at baffled lust, finished in most malignant spite.

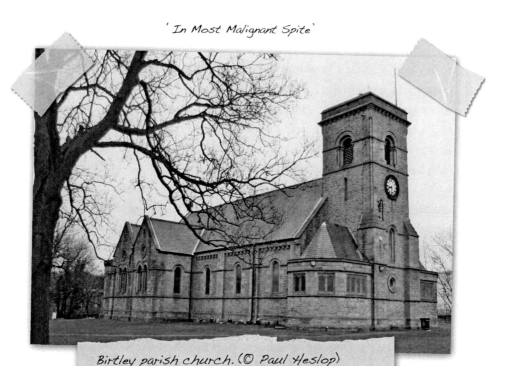

Birtley parish church. (© Paul Heslop)

In us, whose manhood is disgraced, pity for the wretched murderer has a hard struggle with shame at his crime. We will try to say, "May he find mercy", though he showed none.'

A few days after the crime, people began to doubt that Waddle was the culprit, saying that it was not unknown for him to disappear and that his doing so was mere coincidence. Others were worried that the real murderer was 'lurking about'; a suspicious man had been seen in the Birtley area three times since the murder. Two street singers composed a song, which they sang to the accompaniment of a banjo at Pelton Fell, Ouston and Birtley:

> As we the papers read, the news of some dark deed
> Of murder or of outrage meets the eye;
> And scarcely one clear day now seems to pass away
> E're violence claims its victim thus to die.
> Right from London to the North, a cry it has gone forth
> Of indignation at these brutal crimes;
> And now we have to tell of one at Birtley Fell
> As black a deed as e'er disgraced our times.

William Waddle's location was still a mystery even with all the public interest. At seven o'clock on the Sunday morning (the same day Jane's body was found) he was at Corbridge asking for directions. It transpired that he had a brother living there and he was trying to find him. He would later be described as looking as if he had been out all night – which he undoubtedly had, having probably walked the 25 miles from Birtley.

On Thursday, having traversed Northumberland, Waddle turned up at a broker's shop in Berwick-upon-Tweed, where he was served by a Mrs Brodie. He asked for an exchange of clothing and some money. He was still wearing the suit of clothes he wore when last seen at Birtley. Mrs Brodie provided him with a coat, fustian trousers, and a vest, and paid him 5s. He asked her for food and she gave him some. He then asked for a cap, but as she was unable to provide one he left the shop and entered another where he bought a cap for 6d. He now had a complete change of clothing.

On Monday 1 October he was at Spittal near Berwick, where he was seen on the road by Police Constable James Frizzel. Waddle told the policeman that he was William Lee from Otterburn and that he was looking for harvest work. The constable, satisfied that he had told the truth, allowed him to go on his way. Whether this encounter sparked greater police activity in the area is not known, but shortly afterwards, Constable Thomas Smith went to Mrs Brodie's shop and she handed him the clothes she had taken from Waddle. Meanwhile, Waddle wandered into Scotland, where on a lonely road near Kirk Yetholm he met William Stenhouse, a wool dealer, who thought he answered the description of the man wanted for the murder of the woman on Tyneside.

Waddle told Stenhouse that he came from Coldstream. He was encouraged to name several persons there, which he did. Stenhouse had heard of none of them. He invited Waddle to accompany him, saying he would find him harvest work. Stenhouse then asked him outright if his name was William Waddle. 'No,' replied Waddle, 'it's William Laws.' When had he left Birtley? 'Sunday morning,' said Waddle. Did he know a woman named Savage? 'Yes, that is my wife,' Waddle replied. Stenhouse then escorted Waddle to the police station in Kirk Yetholm, where he told him he was his prisoner and he was going to 'lock him up'. Waddle offered no resistance and Stenhouse locked him in a cell pending the arrival of Police Constable John Thompson, who was scouring the countryside looking for Waddle when he got the call.

Waddle told PC Thomson that his name was Laws and denied that he came from Birtley. The constable then handed his notebook to Waddle, telling him to write his name in it. Waddle wrote: 'William Waddle, Birtley Brickyard'. Having been a fugitive on the road for nearly a week, he was undoubtedly exhausted and probably unable to focus on what he was doing. He was hungry and unkempt; when he appeared before the magistrates at Gateshead the next day he was described as an 'abject and pitiful sight', leaning on the rail of the dock with his head sunk into his chest. But if his appearance was wretched, he never once admitted to the crime.

'Portrait of William Waddle'. An artist's impression of how he appeared in the magistrates' court. (Author's collection)

When he next appeared before the magistrates at Chester-le-Street, he maintained a keen interest in proceedings, pleading 'not guilty' to the charge of murder. There would never be any direct evidence to connect him with the murder of Jane Beardmore, nor was the murder weapon ever found. There were some bloodstains on the clothing recovered from the shop in Berwick, but there was no proof that the blood was Jane's, or that it was even human.

William Waddle appeared at the Durham Assizes in November. The judge, Baron Pollock, did not mince his words, telling the jury at the outset that he thought they would have 'no difficulty with regard to the conclusion to which they should come'. His Lordship said that Waddle had been a 'decent, respectable and quiet man' who had paid attentions to 'the girl' for some time and was in the habit of 'walking out with her'. Mr Steavenson, for the prosecution, outlined the facts before calling, among other witnesses, miner Thomas Falloon. Falloon told the court that a week before the murder he 'exchanged' knives with Waddle, and a knife was produced in court made by the same manufacturer. It was a pity, observed his Lordship, to show any witness a knife that was not actually part of the evidence. 'Better put the knife aside,' he said, and 'let the witness describe it instead'. Falloon did so, explaining that the initials 'J.F.' were inscribed on one side of the handle on the knife he had given to Waddle. But the knife to which he referred, by implication the murder weapon, had not been found. All his 'evidence' amounted to was that he had given a knife to Waddle and indeed, it would have been difficult to have found a working man who *didn't* have a knife.

After half an hour of deliberation, the jury found Waddle guilty of murder. After being sentenced to death 'in the usual form', he stood mute and expressionless, as if he had not heard. His Lordship concluded by expressing his admiration of the 'shrewd acumen and public spirit' displayed by William Stenhouse, who, alone on a lonely road, had arrested Waddle – a man he believed could be armed with a knife. He ordered 'a payment of money' to be made to Stenhouse 'from the pockets of ratepayers'.

William Waddle stood convicted of a barbaric murder, but was his conviction right? There was no forensic evidence to link him with the crime scene and no murder weapon proved to be in his possession was ever found. He never admitted to the crime. And yet can there be any doubt that he was guilty? His conduct – drunk and surly – on the evening in question, his sudden, unannounced disappearance from home and employment, lying about his identity, changing clothes in a shop in Berwick; the circumstantial evidence was overwhelming. As to motive, Waddle acquiring a knife before the deed may indicate an early intent to kill the woman he called his sweetheart if she rejected him.

It is worth reflecting on the actions of PC Dodds, who attended the scene of the crime and promptly had the body removed. This differs from today's procedure, where a scene is protected and forensically examined. Yet in times before blood grouping and DNA, PC Dodds' actions hardly mattered. Even so, one would have thought some sort of examination of the scene might have been made before moving the body. Finally, regarding the judge's commendation of William Stenhouse, who placed Waddle in a cell pending

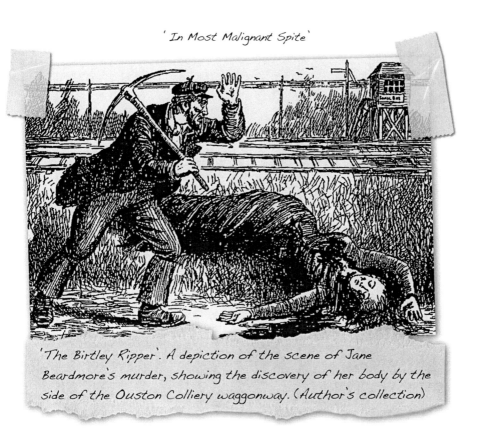

'The Birtley Ripper'. A depiction of the scene of Jane Beardmore's murder, showing the discovery of her body by the side of the Ouston Colliery waggonway. (Author's collection)

the arrival of a constable, he could be liable for false imprisonment or assault if he did so today.

Just before eight o'clock on 18 December 1888, 'a dull and misty morning', William Waddle was taken from his cell in Durham Gaol to begin his fateful walk to the gallows. To the 'mournful toll' of the prison bell he stood on the trapdoors and the executioner, James Berry, placed the white cap over his head and pulled the lever. Death was reported as instant. The previous execution to have happened there was that of Joseph Lowson (of the previous case, hanged for the murder of Sergeant William Smith), which had been public and had drawn a huge crowd. William Waddle's execution was attended by a mere handful of people gathered outside the prison walls to see the black flag raised, signifying punishment had been carried out. In the city itself folk went about their business as though nothing had happened.

Buoyed up by the Love of a Woman

Gateshead, 1910

Suspect: Thomas Craig

Age: 24

Charge: Murder

Sentence: Execution

Sentenced to seven years' imprisonment for housebreaking and grievous bodily harm, Thomas Craig at least had one thing to sustain him: his sweetheart, Annie Finn, had sworn that she would wait for him. Indeed, as time passed, it seemed that she would keep her word, but then came the letter from Annie's sister, Winifred. It was bad news; Annie had met someone else and had agreed to marry him.

Craig had met Annie in 1903 at Barnard Castle when he was doing military training. Now, in early 1910, after serving nearly six years of his sentence, she was jilting him. So, on 4 January he wrote to Annie. The letter (abridged) read, 'You will see with sorrow when I come, as you will go to ware [sic] your mother is as you no [know] that Sally Shaw'. Annie's mother and Sally Shaw were both dead. The letter went on, 'You will be like her in a few weeks' time next month as my flesh and blood cannot stand this ... I'll come like death itself ... You have only to die once, as I am not afraid to die and face death. Your happiness will be short. I will forgive you if you are still Annie Finn, but if you are not God help you and to your mother you will go like a flash'.

Annie was married to a glass worker named Thomas William Henderson, aged twenty-two, on 5 February. Craig was released from Portland Gaol in Dorset just a few weeks later on 24 March and he went in search of her. The very next day he went to Barnard Castle, where Winifred Finn told him Annie was married. He told her, 'If I had met her instead [of you] she would have no husband to go back to.' He asked for Annie's address, but not surprisingly Winifred refused to give it to him. Craig, in tears, told her he knew she was in Newcastle or Gateshead and he would search the streets there until he found her.

'Look here, Tommy, I have had plenty of trouble these last five years, we'll have no more,' said Winifred.

On 26 March, Craig went to Crook where he saw Thomas Priestman who was married to another of Annie's sisters. 'Where does Annie live?' asked Craig.

'I don't know,' said Priestman, but he knew someone who did. He took him to see a man named Harrison who told Craig that Annie and her husband lived in Gateshead, and gave him an address which Craig wrote down on the back of an envelope.

'If I had known the game that was going on I would have twisted his [expletive unknown] neck,' Craig told Priestman, meaning Annie's husband. Craig asked Priestman about trains to Gateshead.

'*In search of Annie Finn*'. *The Market Cross, Barnard Castle. (© Paul Heslop)*

'Write to me when you get home,' Priestman said.

'I may never get the chance to write,' Craig told him.

Craig wasted no time and at 2 p.m. that same day he turned up at Pape's gunmakers in Collingwood Street, Newcastle. He told the shopkeeper, Thomas Simpson, that he wished to purchase a revolver to protect his property and gave his name as John Wilson of 1 North Road, Durham, and that as a 'householder' had the right to purchase a firearm. Simpson sold him a revolver and fifty cartridges. Craig then crossed the Tyne into Gateshead, where he approached stranger William Tait in the street and asked him if he 'knew where Tommy Henderson that works in the glass-house lived'. Tait said he did and would show him the way, accompanying Craig to Oakwellgate. On the way, Craig caught sight of two policemen and asked Tait to get in front of him, saying, 'I got pinched this morning for gambling,' and stepped into the nearby Brewery Yard. After the policemen had gone, Tait led Craig to the house of Mrs Mary Henderson, Tommy Henderson's mother.

Craig asked Mrs Henderson if her son lived there and she replied that he did not. Craig explained that he was a cousin of Annie Henderson, so she led him to her son's house in nearby Carter's Yard. Her son and his wife were in the kitchen when Craig entered the house and sat by the door. Upon seeing him, Annie Henderson said, 'You're Tommy Craig, aren't you?'

'Aye,' he replied, 'and you're Annie Finn.'

Annie said, 'I am Mrs Henderson now, and this is my husband.' Tommy Henderson went to shake hands with Craig, who ignored him.

'Why did you throw me over?' he asked her.

'Because I loved my husband best,' she replied. Tommy Henderson then stood on a chair and began to hang a picture on the wall, and Mrs Henderson senior went into a bedroom.

Annie, who had received Craig's letter of 4 January and was aware of his threats, sat down on the sofa with her back to Craig. Suddenly, there was a pistol shot and Tommy Henderson, jumping from the chair, cried out, 'Oh Annie!' Craig then shot Annie.

Mary Henderson rushed into the kitchen to find her daughter-in-law had been wounded in the chest and her son had been shot in the back. The room was now filled with acrid smoke. Craig then fired two shots at her, both missing, whereupon he began chasing her around the table. She ran into the scullery and Craig, pointing the gun at her, suddenly ran out of the house pursued by the mortally-wounded Tommy Henderson.

Neighbours heard the shots, and saw Craig and Henderson run up a narrow lane. Craig escaped but Henderson, apparently thinking he had turned down the street, headed in that direction. He reached the High Street where he fell through loss of blood and exhaustion, he was taken to the nearby police station where he was examined by Dr Charles West, but died about twenty minutes later. Cause of death would later be ascribed to the bullet having penetrated his back below the right shoulder blade, splintering two ribs and entering a lung. The police found a spent cartridge in Maiden's Walk, which suggested that Craig had made his way into Newcastle across the Swing Bridge, throwing cartridges away as he went.

Annie Henderson was taken to the Newcastle Royal Infirmary, where the bullet was extracted from her right breast. She survived the murder attempt. Craig disappeared, whereabouts unknown.

At the subsequent inquest into the death of Thomas Henderson, the coroner said 'a more heartless, cold-blooded and cruel murder could hardly be committed', and that was before the coroner's jury had returned their verdict – one of wilful murder against Thomas Craig, whose apprehension was demanded on a warrant which the coroner handed to the chief constable of Gateshead Borough Police, James Trotter.

Thomas Craig was armed and on the run, but even fugitives have to eat and this was his ultimate undoing. There was a burglary at a farmhouse near Ovingham in Northumberland, where food was stolen. A sighting led police to Healey Woods near Riding Mill, which they searched without success. Then there were two burglaries at Dilston Hall near Corbridge, Northumberland, as well as a nearby farm, on 11 and 12 April, this time with food and liquor being stolen. On Friday, 15 April reports of a 'suspicious character' reached police at Gateshead and six officers from the borough force, assisted by those from the Northumberland County area, went to Dilston first thing the following morning.

After first searching unsuccessfully, they came to Dilston Cottage Farm where officers entered a cowshed. Constable Reed of the Gateshead force went up into a hayloft and almost immediately called down, 'There is a bag here.' The farmer was quick to say there wasn't, whereupon PC Reed declared, 'It's a man!' It was Thomas Craig, who was asleep; and just as well, for when he was searched the revolver was found in his trouser pocket and it was loaded. Craig offered slight resistance and was arrested. He had food and cigarettes in his possession, along with two stolen coats and partly consumed bottles of spirits, which were hidden in the hay. He also had the letters that Annie had written to him whilst in prison. Later, the cartridges found in his possession would be compared to the one found in Maiden's Way and discovered to be match.

In custody Craig admitted he had found whatever food he could, as well as begging for money. He had walked far and wide: to Chester-le-Street, from where he had intended to go to Scotland. Five times he headed for Scotland, but somehow missed the road and on each occasion ended up at Consett. He said the previous evening he had stolen a bicycle from Dilston Hall and practised riding it through the night, with the intention of cycling to Scotland, but had given up and had returned the bicycle. He admitted breaking into a cottage near Corbridge, where a woman lay asleep on the sofa and a man lay in bed upstairs. He raided the pantry where he stole meat, bread and vegetables, which he ate at the kitchen table before walking 'gently' from the house, closing the door behind him. In another house he found a newspaper in which he read that he had not killed Annie, but that Thomas Henderson had died through being shot. He told police that he was sorry and that he only had intended to 'wing' him.

Craig was taken by train to the Central Railway Station in Newcastle, and from there by taxi across the High Level Bridge to Gateshead. The news of his capture had spread, and as the taxi carrying Craig and police officers emerged from

Dilston Hall, Northumberland. Thomas Craig committed burglaries here when on the run from the police, probably to steal food. (© Paul Heslop)

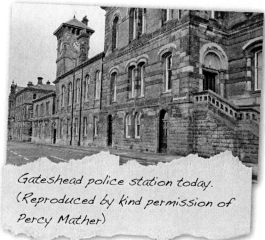

Gateshead police station today.
(Reproduced by kind permission of
Percy Mather)

the High Level Bridge a crowd followed it to the police station and hooted at Craig when he left the vehicle. Someone shouted, to the police, 'Good luck, you've got him now.' In the case notes it is recorded that he was 'given a bath' before being placed into a cell. One wonders for whose benefit that was.

Thomas Craig was charged with the murder of Thomas Henderson and appeared before the magistrates on 23 April, where he was additionally charged with causing grievous bodily harm to Annie Henderson. He stood trial before Justice Grantham at Durham Assizes in June and pleaded 'not guilty' to murder. The charge of grievous bodily harm against Annie Henderson was not proceeded with. Mr Bruce Williamson, for the prosecution, outlined the facts to the jury. When Sergeant Hall testified, he said that when charged with the murder Craig had replied, 'I did not intend to kill the man. I intended to kill Annie and then myself. The reason I did not kill myself was because I did not see Annie drop.' Alluding to the occasion when he had been sentenced to seven years' imprisonment, he said, 'I meant to shoot Justice Darling [the trial judge] but I could not find out where he lived when I came out of Portland.'

Called by Mr Griffith-Jones, for the defence, Craig's father said that in the year of his son's birth 'his mother was not right in her mind'. Griffith-Jones urged the jury to find Craig guilty of manslaughter rather than murder, saying that the provocation caused by being 'thrown over' by the girl he loved acted seriously on a weak mind. Though only twenty-four, his mind had for several years been 'buoyed up' by the love of this woman and her promise to marry him.

Summing up, his Lordship said it would be lamentable if anyone took the law into their own hands simply because he was annoyed at having been jilted, or because a judge had given him a long term of imprisonment. He said there was no evidence to show there was anything wrong with Craig's mind and that he was as sane as anyone. There was not a more determined man in the world than Craig had shown himself to be. The jury found him guilty as charged, with a recommendation to mercy.

Asked if he had anything to say, Craig replied, 'I am quite willing to face death, sir.' His Lordship, having assumed the black cap, described Craig's actions as murder under the most shocking circumstances. 'A man just married to a girl to whom the prisoner was devoted, his life taken from him in revenge and jealousy. This opens out a vista to society if such a crime could be for a moment tolerated. He not only murdered the man but he intended to murder his wife.' He said he could see 'no hope' that the jury's recommendation to mercy would have any effect. He sentenced Craig to death. Leaving the dock, Craig waved to someone, a gesture that drew forth a 'low murmur of sympathy from a female'.

One might hardly think anyone would have sympathy for Thomas Craig, but his friends in his home town of Spennymoor got up a petition of 5,000 names, which was sent to the Home Secretary, Winston Churchill, asking for leniency. But by the date of his execution on 12 July, no word of reprieve came. Craig rose at 7 a.m. and was attended by the Revd Canon Brown, the Roman Catholic chaplain of the prison, who remained with him until the end. Prison warders were sent to bring Craig from his cell to the doctor's room, where he was pinioned by executioner Pierrepoint and taken to the scaffold on his 'last earthly journey'. Craig walked firmly without assistance and no sooner had he positioned himself on the drop than Pierrepoint bound his ankles, placed the noose around his neck and pulled the white cap over his head. He then pulled the lever, releasing the bolt, and Thomas Craig 'shot down' into the cavity below. Death was reported as instantaneous. As the clock struck eight o'clock, the prison bell sounded on the fourth stroke, signalling that the execution had been carried out. Throughout the entire proceedings Craig never spoke a word. He was the thirty-fourth murderer to be hanged at Durham Gaol.

Should Thomas Craig have been shown mercy, as the jury asked? At one of the magistrates' court hearings, the prosecuting solicitor described his actions as 'wanton murder, evidently the outcome of unbridled passion'. Passion maybe, but the coroner surely got it right when he described Craig's actions as 'heartless', 'cold-blooded' and 'cruel'. Whether driven by love, jealousy, revenge or unbridled passion, purchasing a firearm, seeking out his victims, shooting two people and trying to shoot a third amounted to all of those things.

SOLVED

Murder on the Railway

Lintz Green, 1911

Suspect: Samuel Atkinson

Age: 25

Charge: Murder

Sentence: Acquitted

Sixty-year-old widower George Wilson was stationmaster at Lintz Green near Burnopfield, and would have been looking forward to retirement after forty years with the North Eastern Railway. A former signalman, he had been promoted to stationmaster at Langley on the Allendale line and had been in his present post for nine years.

Wilson was a man of quiet disposition, a teetotaller, a Methodist, and a conscientious railwayman who, in addition to his duties, applied his gardening talents to the station garden, winning prizes for the best-kept station on the Newcastle–Consett line. The station was situated in a quiet location, surrounded by trees and not accessible by road. It was a seemingly unlikely location for murder.

As stationmaster, it was Wilson's practice to make up the cash for the day at about eight or nine o'clock every evening and carry it into his house situated near to the station platform, for safekeeping. Sometimes he did not take it until the last train had gone, but on Saturdays he invariably took the cash home at about eight o'clock. Consequently, on the night of Saturday, 7 October 1911 he took the day's takings to his house at that time.

The money was carried in a small leather bag, designed for that purpose, and secured by a brass padlock.

The last train that day was the 10.32 from Newcastle to Consett, although it was running ten minutes late. On its arrival there were three railwaymen on duty at the station: Wilson himself, a porter named Routledge and Frederick White, the booking clerk-cum-ticket collector. Routledge left the station on the train when it departed for Consett a few minutes later.

Four passengers alighted at Lintz Green. They were Samuel Elliott, Robert Wailes and Thomas Middleton, all of whom had travelled from Newcastle, and a man named Charles Swinburne, a friend of White. Elliott, Wailes and Middleton crossed the tracks to walk to their homes at Low Friarside about half a mile away. Meanwhile, having spoken to the guard and the train having departed, Wilson crossed the tracks to go to his house, carrying a lantern to light his way. White, having collected the tickets from the three passengers, extinguished the lights, leaving the entire station in darkness.

Wilson lived with his twenty-four-year-old daughter, Bertha, who acted as his housekeeper. She was upstairs in bed expecting her father's imminent arrival. There was a candle burning at the stairhead window for her father to see when he came in and at about a 10.45 p.m. she heard a 'slight noise', which she thought was 'furniture cracking'. Then she heard a scuffling noise outside, followed by a shot.

Betha went at once to the stairhead window and shouted to her father, 'Are you hurt? What's the matter?'

Her father called back, 'Oh yes. Oh yes.'

She shouted, 'I'm coming,' and ran downstairs. Just inside the door she called out, 'Is there anybody there?' but there was no answer. She shouted loudly, 'Dad, are you there?' She thought he might have said something, and then she screamed.

Fred White, the booking clerk, also heard the shot. He went directly towards the house with Charles Swinburne. White saw Bertha at the door with a light. 'Oh Fred,' cried Bertha, 'there is something happened to father. See what it is!' White found Wilson lying on the ground among the shrubbery.

'Come away in,' he called out to Bertha. Elliott, Wailes and Middleton, all of whom had heard Bertha's scream and the shot, then arrived. The men carried Wilson into the house and laid him on a couch. Middleton, an ambulance man, loosened Wilson's tie and collar and gave him brandy. Wilson tried to speak, but he could only gurgle. A few moments later he died.

When Bertha opened the door she saw something lying on the doorstep, which turned out to be a piece of cloth containing sand, probably meant to be a cosh. Nearby was a piece of linen, knotted in the centre with strings attached, which might have been intended as a gag. The police were called and attended under the supervision of Superintendent Dryden of Consett. Having established that George Wilson had been shot at close range, they searched the area but found no trace of his assailant or a weapon. It would have seemed obvious that the motive for the killing was robbery, but the murderer had probably mistimed his attack in the belief that Wilson was carrying the day's receipts to his house when the last train left the station. Nevertheless, although his timing was wrong, the fact that he evidently thought Wilson was carrying cash would lend weight to the theory that the murderer knew something of the habits of the stationmaster. Wilson had £13 10s in his pocket, but his killer did not linger to search him for personal cash.

Dr Boland arrived at the scene at half-past midnight and examined the body in situ; he found a wound on the left side of the chest, between the fifth and sixth ribs. The bullet had passed through George Wilson's chest and exited through his back, and it was recovered near a wall that it had struck. Boland later carried out a post-mortem examination, and at the inquest held in the ladies' waiting room at the station on the Monday he told the jury that Wilson had been shot through the heart. He also said that sand had been thrown into Wilson's eyes, confirming that the motive was almost certainly robbery.

The coroner, Mr Graham, asked George Wilson's uncle, Thomas Shotton, to tell Miss Wilson 'We are all very deeply grieved for her, and sympathise from our heart with her ... and we shall do our best to investigate the matter, and we hope the criminal or criminals responsible for this dreadful outrage will be brought to justice'. George Wilson was buried next to his late wife in St James' churchyard in Burnopfield on the Tuesday afternoon.

Meanwhile, the *Durham Chronicle* voiced the opinion that there was a 'strong impression' that even though George Wilson had been partially blinded by sand being thrown into his eyes, 'He recognised his assailant or

Lintz Green Railway Station about the time of the murder of stationmaster Joseph Wilson. The station closed in 1953 with the demise of the Derwent Valley railway. (Reproduced by permission of Durham County Record Office, Ref. D/X 1611/23/11/2)

assailants, as it is now believed that *two persons* were implicated, and that he would have disclosed their identity had he been able to speak before he died'. It is unknown how the newspaper acquired the apparent evidence to suggest that there were two assailants.

This was a difficult case for the police, as George Wilson had no known enemies, and if the motive for his murder was robbery, where could they begin to look? There were no witnesses to the killing, and they did not find the murder weapon, so were unable to check for fingerprints. Nevertheless, on 12 October, five days after the crime, they made an arrest. The suspect was Samuel Atkinson, a twenty-five-year-old single man who lived with his parents at Byker in the east end of Newcastle. Atkinson was employed as a 'casual porter' by the railway company, and on the day of the crime had been on duty at Lintz Green station, finishing work at 3.45 p.m. He went home, but was reportedly seen again on the station platform later that same day, being there 'just about the time the last train came in'. Two witnesses told police that Atkinson was the man they saw at the station, one was positive and the other said he was like a man he saw there.

At nine o'clock on the night of Wednesday 11 October, Inspector Gargate and Sergeant Tait of Consett, accompanied by officers from Newcastle City Police, went to Kirk Street in Byker. They were told by family members that Atkinson was not at home, but the officers went in and found him upstairs in bed. He was taken to the next room and spoken to alone, and asked to account for his movements the previous Saturday. Atkinson said he had left the station just before four o'clock, when he went home. He said, 'I remained in the house till about seven o'clock, when I had a walk into the Bigg Market [in Newcastle city centre]. I only saw one man, whom I know by sight. I do not know his name or where he lives, but he is a casual porter on the North Eastern Railway, the same as myself.' The officers decided the answers to their questions were 'unsatisfactory' and arrested him. He was taken to Consett police station on suspicion of the murder of George Wilson and was later charged.

At Consett Police Court the next morning, Superintendent Dryden requested he be remanded in custody pending further enquiries. Asked if he had any objection, Atkinson said, 'I do not think it should be so. I have done no harm. I cannot see why I should be remanded. I can bring plenty of witnesses to show where I was on Saturday night.'

Superintendent Dryden said Atkinson had had every opportunity of telling police his movements on the night in question, but did not give any 'definite evidence' as to 'what he did or where he was or whom he met'. Atkinson was remanded for a week. When he next appeared before the magistrates he was represented by solicitor Edward Clark. Photographers were excluded from the court and a senior policeman, Superintendent Brock, addressed the 'large array of pressmen'. 'Are any of you gentlemen artists?' he enquired, and after getting no response told them, 'If there are artists amongst you I should like to say it is very important that no photographs or sketch of the prisoner should be taken at this stage of the proceedings. You will understand that if the accused's portrait is published it might lead people to think they could identify him, when otherwise they would not have been able to do so. It would be very unfair to the prisoner.'

When Atkinson appeared in court, according to the *Newcastle Daily Journal*, he 'seemed to be in the best of health' as he faced the magistrates.

Inspector Gargate said that on 11 October he and other officers went to 138 Kirk Street in Byker and saw Atkinson, and Gargate was about to give a statement that he said had been made by Atkinson when Mr Clark interjected, saying, 'This was not a voluntary statement and cannot be given in evidence.' Superintendent Brock said that Atkinson was not a suspect at the time he made the statement, that he was 'one of many interviewed at Newcastle about the murder', which is why he was not cautioned at that time.

It seems Mr Clark's objection was upheld, for Atkinson's statement, whatever it was, was not heard. Instead, Inspector Gargate simply told the court that Atkinson was arrested and brought to Consett the following day. Superintendent Dryden then told the court, 'He was placed with a dozen other men in the yard, and three men picked him out as being like the man ...' The court was not told about any details of an identification parade, nor of the identification of the 'three men'. Their identity is a mystery, since no evidence was ever forthcoming of the murderer being seen at the scene of the crime. It may be Atkinson was 'identified' as being seen elsewhere, thus refuting his alibi about being in the Bigg Market – but this is mere conjecture.

Superintendent Dryden then declared, 'On this evidence I ask for a remand [in custody] to enable us to conclude enquiries which are incomplete.' There did not seem to be any other evidence than that they had made an arrest. The court had not heard of any admissions of guilt, nor of any other evidence incriminating Atkinson to any degree. 'There is not a tittle of evidence of any sort implicating this man,' said Mr Clark, 'but because I think it is beneficial to the man himself that the fullest enquiries should be made, I consent to him being remanded without evidence.' The magistrates again remanded Atkinson to Durham Gaol.

Six days later, Atkinson was taken from Durham Gaol to the superintendent's office at Durham police station, where Mr W. Morant, for the Director of Public Prosecutions, told the magistrate, Captain Apperley, that he had been instructed to offer no further evidence, and asked him to 'discharge the prisoner'. Mr Clark naturally offered no objection but asked that a payment of money be made to Atkinson, saying 'the poor man had been put to a good deal of expense in preparation of his defence'. He pointed out that the court had the power to pay up to £25. However, after some argument and although Atkinson was dismissed, this application was refused.

Durham Assize Courts in 1929. The chimneys of Durham Gaol appear behind. Formerly a 'hanging prison', executions took place here between 1869, the last being a serving soldier hanged for 'committing murder in the furtherance of theft' in 1958. (Reproduced by permission of Durham County Record Office, Ref. D/CL 5/829)

On 11 November the police went to Barlow near Winlaton and arrested another man on suspicion of the murder, who worked at a gunsmith's shop in Newcastle. He was taken to Blaydon police station and placed in an identification parade where a 'witness' failed to identify him. A reward of £100 'to be paid by the North Eastern Railway Company' was then offered for information in 'respect of the Lintz Green murder'. The reward notice included details of a man aged twenty to twenty-two years old, who walked with a slight stoop, 'having the appearance of one used to living in a country district', who had purchased a box of fifty revolver cartridges at a gunsmith's shop in Newcastle on the day of the murder. Alas to no avail. The murder of stationmaster George Wilson was never solved.

Case Ten

A Savage and Ferocious Beast

Ferryhill, 1928

Suspect: Norman Elliott

Age: 22

Charge: Murder

Sentence: Execution

Thursday, 16 February 1928 would have been another routine day in the life of thirty-one-year-old William Byland Abbey, a cashier at Lloyds Bank in Ferryhill. That morning, Mr Abbey went to the bank as usual, where he worked alone and was in charge of a 'good deal' of money; a situation that was of ongoing concern to the Bank Officers' Guild (the bank employees' trade union) but not to Lloyds, whose representative would say that 'If anyone had suggested that murder could take place at the bank in Ferryhill, the ordinary commonsense man would have said it was impossible'.

Unlikely it may have been, but impossible it was not, for Mr Abbey was attacked at his post at three o'clock – closing time. He was brutally attacked by a man who struck him with several blows to the head with a heavy instrument before stabbing him twice in the neck with a cobbler's knife, grabbing what money he could and running into the street, where he made his escape. Despite being mortally wounded, Abbey was able to pick up a heavy paperweight and throw it through the window, shattering the glass to attract the attention of passers-by who rushed into the bank where they found him staggering behind the counter with blood pouring from his neck.

As they helped him to sit down, he was heard to say, 'It was a tall man who did it.' He died at his post shortly afterwards.

As the police hunted for Abbey's killer, the inquest into his death was opened at the Institute in Ferryhill. The coroner, Mr J.T. Proud, told the jury that thanks to an alteration in the law they would be spared the 'unpleasant duty' of viewing the body, but he said Mr Abbey must have put up a good fight, as his injuries showed there had been 'very great violence' and that his assailant had had a 'fixed intent to plunder and rob, and must have become a ferocious wild beast'.

On the following Monday afternoon, Abbey was interred in Ferryhill cemetery, after a service that was held next to the War Memorial in the Market Place which 'fully six thousand from ten miles radius' attended. Those present were unlikely to suspect that even as Abbey's funeral was being conducted the police were arresting twenty-two-year-old Norman Elliott, a night attendant at the County Asylum at Winterton, near Sedgefield.

Information about Elliott had been passed to the police by a Stockton traveller who knew him and had seen and spoken to him at Ferryhill on the afternoon of the crime. Until recently, Elliott had been living at Spennymoor,

The Black Bull, Ferryhill – once the premises of Lloyds Bank, where William Byland Abbey was murdered. (Author's collection)

but a month before the crime had married Elizabeth Callan, whose parents lived at the Turk's Head public house at Kelloe.

The police, having first gone to Spennymoor, went on to Kelloe Colliery and waited for Elliott to alight from a bus which called at the village. He was taken to the Turk's Head where he and his wife were living, although they were preparing to move into a rented room nearby.

Elliott had 'honourable connections' with the police force. His father was a former constable at Moorsley near Hetton but had become depressed after his wife's death, and later committed suicide on a railway line; Elliott's late grandfather was a former inspector who had served at Tudhoe Colliery and Spennymoor. One imagines that both men would have been mortified had they known that Norman had not only been arrested on suspicion of murder, but was quickly charged and appeared before the county magistrates

The War Memorial, Ferryhill. 'Fully six thousand from a ten mile radius' attended the service here, held in memory of William Byland Abbey. (© Paul Heslop)

at Durham. 'Wearing a fashionably cut brown overcoat and conspicuous yellow and black tie', Elliott was described by the press as the best dressed man in court, which itself would have been remarkable considering that just before his arrest he had no money, a pregnant wife to support and wore boots with holes in the soles.

The court heard that the money stolen from Lloyds bank amounted to the sum of £202 15s 8d and included a cheque 'for a big amount'. They also heard that Mr Abbey had been stabbed in the neck and 'blood had flowed freely from him to the floor'. Mr Abbey had been struck by several blows to the head before being stabbed to death by two thrusts of the knife which had been found nearby, the second thrust proving fatal and severing vital arteries.

The prosecution said that Elliott did not have an account at the bank and had no legitimate reason to be there. He had received some money 'some time ago', when on the death of his father £35 was placed into his credit in the Durham County Police Mutual Association. But from July 1927 he had had no banking transactions. He maintained he had funds, even though he was walking around in boots with holes and was not paying money to his wife for upkeep.

A bus driver and conductress said Elliott got on their bus at Kelloe at about 1.20 p.m. on the day of the crime, and alighted at Thinford crossroads, a mile north of Ferryhill. A witness, Edith Dyke, said she had entered the bank at Ferryhill and saw a man whom she 'definitely identified' as Elliott standing behind the counter – but she had failed to pick him out at an identification parade because 'she was too ill to do it'. Another witness, Lazenby Gates, who did not know Elliott, did pick him out. Another man, John William Heavisides, failed to do so.

Roy Barker said he had known Elliott for years and that at 3.30 p.m. on the day of the crime he had seen him walking towards the bottom of Durham Bank in Ferryhill, towards Thinford. Elliott, he said, was 'quite normal'. Gladys Turner said that at about 4 p.m. he boarded her bus again at Metal Bridge, a mile east of Thinford crossroads. She reproached him for not speaking to her earlier in Ferryhill, to which he replied, 'You are making a mistake. I have not been in Ferryhill today.'

If the identification of Elliott as the murderer was uncertain, other evidence was more supportive. James Lockhead worked at the asylum with Elliott and said that on 9 February he gave Elliott his paynote for £3 2s 10d to be cashed, but two days later Elliott said he had lost the money and his own as well. Yet on Friday 17 February, the day after the crime, Elliott returned his money. It may not sound much today, but it was a week's wages. Ada Grey, head laundress at the asylum, said that on the Monday Elliott handed her a shirt to be laundered which had bloodstains on the right sleeve inside the cuff. She showed the shirt to the matron who then handed it to the police.

The day after the crime, Elliott showed a man named Clark some paid bills and a bundle of £10 notes. 'How would you like to pay bills like that, and have this money and just been married?' Elliott asked him. He had been splashing money about, trying on suits at Jackson & Sons, Stockton, buying a suit at Alexandre the Tailors. He bought £19 9s 6d worth of furniture at Tudhoe, paying for it with twenty £1 notes. When Sergeant George Fleming found a locked portmanteau under Elliott's bed at the asylum, Elliott reluctantly produced the key and Fleming found it to contain £50 in 10s notes, and £43 in £1 notes. Inspector Walker found £110 in a box belonging to Elliott at the asylum. Elliott said the money was his savings. Walker also found sixty-three 10s notes in the folds of a blanket. 'When I lifted the blanket there was a shower of ten shilling notes,' said Walker, who found other Bank of England notes 'concealed all about the room'. When Elliott was detained he had £16, 11s and 9d in his possession. Some of the recovered notes bore Abbey's handwriting in pencil and one was bloodstained. £158 in cash was found in Elliott's room at Kelloe. All in all, he had more money in his possession than had been reported missing by the bank, but there was a small possibility that he had cashed in the cheque that was stolen alongside the cash. Bloodstained clothing was found in Elliott's room at Kelloe.

When first asked to account for his movements Elliott claimed he had not been in Ferryhill on the day of the murder. Then, when pressed, he said that he had but that he had not been in the bank. He made a statement later when on remand that said he had been in the bank and that he knew who committed the murder. It was a man he had met at racecourses, who had given him good tips that had made him some money. He had had several letters from this man but was unable to say where he lived, or produce the letters.

Elliott said this man was in the bank shortly after closing time and when he (Elliott) went to the door he found it closed. When he pushed the door, however, 'to his astonishment' it opened. As soon as it did he was seized by the man he mentioned, who drew him into the bank and closed the door. The man warned him to be careful about what he said or he would see that Elliott took part of the blame. He said the man's hands were covered in blood and he daubed them down his clothes, before he placed a bundle of Treasury notes into Elliott's pocket. Elliott said he saw Abbey lying in a huddled position on the floor with a knife in his throat. He heard a groan and went around the counter, intending to remove the knife thinking he was dead, but he lost his nerve and left the bank after putting on his overcoat, which he had left on the counter. By then the man had disappeared.

Details were heard of Elliott's poor financial situation, which prompted his wife to write him a note that read, 'For goodness' sake bring me money as I cannot live on air'.

William Byland Abbey's grave, Ferryhill Cemetery. (© Paul Heslop)

The trial was held at Durham in June before Justice MacKinnon. Elliott pleaded 'not guilty' to the charge of murdering William Byland Abbey. Mr Mortimer, for the prosecution, told the jury that although Elliott had been without money a few days before the crime, immediately afterwards money had been found in the rooms at his home and at the asylum, and he had spent money on clothing and furniture. 'Where,' asked counsel, 'did a man in receipt of £1 8 shillings a week get that substantial sum?'

Fifteen-year-old shop assistant Ensor Latheron said he went to the bank for some change at 3.02 p.m. and that Abbey was behind the counter. There was a man standing on the pavement outside and he was still there when he left. He had picked him out of an identification parade as being Elliott.

Dr James Jack gave particulars of the post-mortem examination, saying Abbey's assailant must have 'seized him by the throat' with his left hand then struck five rapid blows on his forehead with a small mallet or hammer, which would have rendered him unconscious. The first blow with the knife struck a bone and the second inflicted the fatal injuries. 'It was a very determined attack,' said the doctor, adding that 'it was meant to kill'. He was asked if would have required a man of great strength to inflict the injuries. 'Not necessarily of great strength, but of great determination,' replied Dr Jack.

After hearing the testimonies of all other witnesses, Elliott stepped into the witness box. 'Did you commit this murder?' he was asked.

The inscription on the cross of Abbey's grave. (© Paul Heslop)

'No, sir,' he replied.

'Do you know who did?'

'Yes,' said Elliott, who again mentioned the man he had encountered in the bank. His name was Sinclair and he had met him in London in 1927, and had gone to Hurst Park races with him. He had made money through betting on horses, thanks to Sinclair, he said.

He then said that he and Sinclair had travelled by bus on 16 February to the crossroads near Ferryhill, where they got off and walked into the town, arriving shortly after two o'clock. Sinclair said he had business and, anticipating trouble, wanted Elliott to go with him. But Elliott instead 'had a walk to the War Memorial'. Later, Sinclair asked him to wait outside the bank, saying he expected to be there by three o'clock. Elliott said he looked in the bank and Mr Abbey spoke to him. They had met several times on the bus and Abbey knew his name. Elliott said a friend was coming to the bank. Some customers came in and Elliott went outside to see if Sinclair was coming. When he returned he was surprised to find the door to the bank closed. He pushed it and it swung open. He saw Sinclair standing with blood running down the front of his clothes.

'Sinclair threatened me,' said Elliott. 'He said if I gave any warning he would "put me into it". He grabbed my overcoat which I had over my right arm. The bloodstains must have got on to my jacket. He pulled me aside, rammed some notes into my pocket and told me to clear off. I heard a groaning and looking over the counter saw Mr Abbey huddled up. I eased him up, and

The Black Bull today. (© Paul Heslop)

realising my position I put on my overcoat and walked out.' He said he then went to the asylum and 'thrust the money into a portmanteau'. He thought of sending it to the police anonymously, but hadn't the nerve.

Not surprisingly, the cross-examination by Mr Mortimer was lengthy. He asked if Elliott knew a murder had been committed. 'Not until I heard the groan,' Elliott replied. But when he saw the body of Mr Abbey dripping with blood? 'I guessed something then.' And he knew what Sinclair had done? 'Quite.' Did it not occur to him to inform the police? 'I was in a funny position. He threatened to put me into it. His word was as good as mine.'

His Lordship then said, 'There were people outside in the street.'

'I had not time to think of that.'

Elliott, said Mr Mortimer, wore boots with holes in the soles. Why, if he had money?

'I wanted the money to set up a house,' replied Elliott. He was asked why he had not paid James Lockhead before the murder if he had money, as he had asserted. 'Because he had been making suggestive remarks,' said Elliott.

Mr Mortimer asked the jury to consider whether there was any evidence at all that Sinclair even existed outside Elliott's imagination. Elliott had been shown 124 photographs by the police and identified one as a man whom, he said, had sat next to him and Sinclair at Lincoln in March, 1927. When the police made enquiries they found this man had been in Durham Prison at the time. Nobody had been able to find Sinclair, said the counsel, adding that the story was so incredible it could only have been invented by a man who was himself involved in the crime. Before the murder he was hard up and afterwards he was in possession of a considerable amount of Treasury notes.

Mr Linsley, for the defence, focused on the question of identification. A number of witnesses had spoken of seeing Elliott or 'someone like him' standing outside the bank at three o'clock that Thursday afternoon. Some had identified him, but not one could say he struck any blow or even associate him with the murder. Few could realise the terrible predicament 'this unfortunate boy' found himself in. Was he not the tool of Sinclair? Could he have committed murder and robbed a bank, an act that could only have been committed by a 'savage and ferocious beast'?

The judge said Elliott had no bank account and no funds after July 1927. Although he did not spell it out he was clearly questioning how he came to have money the day after the murder. He could not pay his colleague the cash he had drawn for him, yet had paid him the day after the crime, when he also bought clothes and furniture. Did Sinclair exist, and was he in Ferryhill on the day of the crime? No one had spoken to or seen a man of such description; no one had spoken to or seen Elliott, other than when he was alone. As to being dragged into the bank, his Lordship asked, 'Is it conceivable that an innocent man would have acted as he did? It is not as though they were alone in some desert with no one at hand.'

It could hardly have come as a surprise when the jury returned a verdict of 'Guilty'. As his Lordship read out the death sentence, Elliot threw back his head and collapsed into the arms of the warder, screaming, 'Oh, mother, mother, mother!', whereupon he was lifted and carried from the dock. Awaiting his fate, he wrote lots of letters to his wife, assuring her of his innocence and that he would escape death. His assurances were in vain and on 10 August 1928 he was hanged in Durham Gaol.

A Scene of Horror

Norton-on-Tees, 1928

Suspect: Charles William
             Conlin

Age: 22

Charge: Murder

Sentence: Execution

On the afternoon of Saturday, 22 September 1928, a woman walking in the Darlington Lane area of Norton noticed a small mound of freshly-dug earth at the side of the path and decided to take a closer look. One can only imagine her feelings when she saw a human hand protruding from the soil. She immediately called the police.

Detective Sergeant Clayton Whittaker attended the scene and could never have anticipated the scene of horror that awaited him. After moving the earth, he discovered the body of a man lying on his back, with blood oozing from a wound on his forehead. The head was resting upon the portion of the coat that covers the shoulders, as though the body had been dragged along the ground. Under Whittaker's supervision the body was removed from its shallow grave – only to reveal a second body underneath – that of a woman. She was fully dressed and it appeared that she too had been dragged along the ground.

Whittaker saw that the man had sustained wounds to the head, and the woman had discoloration to the throat and several scratches on the side of her face. Blood oozed from her throat and there was a wound on the back of her head. The grave, which was 6ft in length, was merely a deepening of the gutter and being shallow would have taken little time to dig. There was blood near the grave and on the footpath. Whittaker found a woman's hat and glove nearby. A spade was found, concealed in a hedge, about 15ft from the grave. Ironically, Whittaker knew the deceased couple. They were Thomas Kirby, aged sixty, and his wife, Emily Francis Kirby, aged sixty-four. Although of retirement age, both were still employed; he was 'helping out' his son, Thomas Kirby, a hardware dealer, whilst Mrs Kirby ran a tripe stall at Stockton market. They had been married just five years and had lived at Briargarth in Old Thornaby about four miles away.

Dr McBean of Stockton examined both bodies at the scene, finding them both warm and estimated that the time of death in each case was between eight and twenty hours previous to their discovery. The bodies were removed to the mortuary.

Detective Sergeant Whittaker went to the Kirbys' home and found 'not the slightest sign of a disturbance'. In the kitchen, breakfast was laid for two and a pan of porridge stood on the fireplace. The porridge had been cooked, but no one had breakfasted at the house.

That evening Dr McBean carried out the post-mortem examinations on the bodies. He thought that the wound on Mr Kirby's head might have been caused by an instrument such as a poker. If death had been instantaneous, said the doctor, there would have been no bleeding, but as bleeding had taken place it was believed that Mr Kirby had not been killed outright. He found grit in the windpipe leading down to a lung, which indicated the man had been breathing when buried, although possibly insensible.

Dr McBean said Mrs Kirby had sustained bruises on her neck, possibly by a hand. Scratches on her face may have been caused by being dragged, face down, across the ground. There was a large swelling to the back of her head as though she had been struck by an object with a flat surface, such as that of a spade. She too had grit down her windpipe. The Kirbys had been brutally attacked and buried alive.

The Kirbys had been financially comfortable. Mrs Kirby had bought a second house on a mortgage and habitually kept considerable sums of money in her handbag. On 18 September, Mr Kirby had received £16 wages and £6 10s rent for a hut at the market, which he kept in a distinctive brown wallet which was given to him as a wedding present. Robbery was a likely motive for the crime.

An old print of Norton-on-Tees. (Author's collection)

Tripe merchant William Brown, who was Mrs Kirby's son by her first husband (she had been widowed), helped his mother at Stockton market, but that Saturday morning he was surprised when his mother never arrived. He was so surprised that he went to the house, only to find it locked. Later that day he saw Mrs Kirby's grandson (his half-nephew), twenty-two-year-old Charles William Conlin, and told him that the Kirbys were missing. He asked Conlin if he could help out and told him to take a lorry to a yard where it was kept. They had a drink, which Conlin paid for, before going off in the lorry.

Conlin had a fiancée and lived at Centenary Crescent in Norton with his sickly mother. He had previously worked for Mrs Kirby, his grandmother, until two years before. At the time of the murder he was employed as a labourer at the Billingham Synthetic Works, but was only part-time and always short of money.

At 2.15 p.m. on the Saturday, the same afternoon as the discovery of the Kirbys' bodies, Conlin, in possession of the lorry, drove to a garage at Norton Green and bought a gallon of petrol. It cost 1*s* and 5*d*. He then drove to Darlington, where he purchased a new pair of shoes in one shop and in another he bought a new suit for 35*s* and 6*d*, as well as a suitcase and a pair of socks. He produced most of the money from a brown leather wallet. Shortly after 5 p.m. that afternoon he bought a second-hand motorcycle at the Duplex garage in Darlington for £21 10s, again producing the money from a brown leather wallet. He gave his particulars as Charles Murphy of 24 Dunning Dykes Road, Edinburgh.

In Darlington he met and introduced himself as Charles Murphy to a young girl called Rose McIntyre. Rose was in town with her friends, and she and Conlin agreed to meet again at 6.45 that evening. Conlin turned up with the motorcycle, which had the suitcase on the back. He took Rose for a ride to Northallerton, with her riding pillion. At Northallerton they went to a hotel, where he had a whisky and she had a port, both of which he paid for. After their drinks they went to the fair, where he bought her a pair of silk stockings, and a tie and handkerchiefs for himself. They returned to Darlington and arranged to meet again at 8.15 the following morning.

Later that Saturday, Conlin drove to Stockton where, just after eleven o'clock that evening, he entered a fish shop owned by Ernest Preston, whom he knew. Preston asked him about his grandparents, remarking that their disappearance was very 'rough'. Conlin turned his head away, and when asked if there was any news he had replied, 'No, I have just come back from Darlington, and have been away all day.' A remark was made that the Kirbys might now be dead, whereupon Conlin abandoned his fish and chip supper and stood up to leave. Preston said he was sorry if what he had said had upset him. Conlin replied, 'I am upset,' and left. It was noticed that on this visit to Stockton Conlin had been wearing new overalls and new gauntlets and, of course, he now had a motorbike.

Meanwhile, the bodies of Mr and Mrs Kirby had been discovered and police enquiries had led them to suspect Conlin as the murderer – his bed had not been slept in on the Friday night and he, together with the lorry he had been asked to drive by William Brown, had disappeared. But there was more.

Firstly, a two-seater car that been parked in Lovers' Lane in Norton on the Friday night was discovered to be stolen. The car was seen being driven from Norton towards Thornaby in the early hours of Saturday morning. Although the driver was not recognised, the police established that he was not the owner of the vehicle. It was later found abandoned about fifty yards from the Kirbys' home in Briargarth at 5 a.m. Mrs Kirby's brown leather handbag, containing a chequebook and five £1 notes, was found nearby.

At 5.30 a.m. Conlin was seen boarding a bus two miles from Briargarth and at 6.10 a.m. he was seen walking along Norton Avenue towards his home.

At 6.20 a.m. he was seen carrying a spade, by a man named Lumsden. Later, when Lumsden happened to see him and asked him what he had been doing 'at that time of the morning', Conlin said that he had 'been walking round Norton' and had not been to bed.

At 7 a.m. Conlin left his home address, having changed his shoes. Later that morning he changed his clothing, then paid 28s and 6d, which he owed to a Mrs Stiff, and boarded the lorry at William Brown's behest. The lorry was later found abandoned in Darlington. Police later discovered Conlin's purchase of the motorcycle and clothing in Darlington, which were all paid for by money taken from a wallet matching the description of Mr Kirby's. A warrant was issued for Conlin's arrest as 'the whole of the resources of the Durham County Police were brought into action and a cordon was drawn around a wide area of the north of England'.

Conlin was last seen on the Saturday night, when he spoke to Ernest Preston in his fish shop. The hunt was on, but Conlin was keeping his appointment with Rose McIntyre at Darlington. They met as they had arranged at 8.15 on the Sunday morning and went for something to eat, before separating and meeting up again at 1.15 p.m.

They then drove to Richmond on the motorcycle and visited a hotel, where he showed her a wallet containing £20, a gold sovereign and some new half-crowns. Rose told him she had not seen the new half-crown, which was of a new design, saying she would like one. Conlin gave one to her, before they set off again on the motorcycle, which broke down at Barton, near Scotch Corner. They continued to Darlington by bus and walked the streets, visiting St Cuthbert's Church. Later, at Conlin's trial, Rose would say they 'had a good time together'.

Conlin and Rose were then seen in Coniscliffe Road, Darlington, by Sergeant John Mitchell. Sergeant Mitchell was joined by Constable James Carr and they approached the couple in High Row. Conlin gave his particulars as Charles Murphy of Albert Road in Darlington, but when asked if he had 'been off on a motorcycle' purchased the previous day at the Duplex Motor Company, he admitted this was correct and he was arrested. When searched he was found to be in possession of £19 – a lot of money for a part-time labourer in 1928, and for which he could not account – and when the clothes he had changed out of were retrieved from his home and sent for examination a large bloodstain was found,

St Cuthbert's Church, Darlington, where Charles Conlin visited before his arrest. (© Paul Heslop)

along with some fur in a pocket of his coat that matched a coat belonging to Mrs Kirby. The wallet he had on his person was also identified as Mr Kirby's. In the police station Conlin was in a state of collapse, saying he 'could not remember anything'. It was a 'perfectly genuine collapse', said Detective Sergeant Whittaker, the policeman who had visited the scene of the crime.

Charles William Conlin stood trial for his life at the Durham Assizes that November, charged with the murders of his grandparents. The *Northern Daily Mail* reported him as being 'A tall young man, almost debonair in appearance, who walked quickly into the dock, gripping the spiked railings and gazing interestedly and anxiously round the court, and wearing a cloth collar with brown tie and a close-fitting suit'. He pleaded 'not guilty'.

Mr Lowenthal, for the prosecution, told the jury that the case was based on circumstantial evidence because 'persons guilty of murder do not commit such crimes in the presence of witnesses'. He said that 'two old people' were found dead on the afternoon on 22 September, buried alive in a shallow grave having first been rendered unconscious. The old woman was induced by the accused to leave her house on the representation that her daughter was ill. 'She was taken in the stolen motor car to Norton where an attempt to strangle her was made. She was then dragged through a hedge into the field and left there. Afterwards the old man was fetched on a similar representation and attacked in the same way, and left in that field after being dragged through the hedge, and both were subsequently buried.' Much of this was conjecture, but was probably somewhere near the truth. Conlin's possession of the murdered man's wallet and having so much money was the 'most damning evidence', he said.

Mr Sykes, for the defence, said no one would ever know what really happened, but pointed out that Conlin's conduct was inconsistent with a 'considering man' who had made no effort to escape. He complained, reasonably, that no doctor had been called to examine him. The jury were invited to consider a defence of insanity, but the judge said he would be 'surprised' if they found Conlin 'fit for a lunatic asylum'. Foolishness and recklessness were not insanity, he said. The jury took three-quarters of an hour to find Conlin guilty. He took the sentence of death 'with much fortitude', but when asked if he had anything to say he was speechless, his gaze fixed upon the judge. For a moment it seemed he might collapse and warders took him by the arm, but he shrugged them off, saying, 'It's alright.' He turned and lingered, looking at the seat that had been occupied throughout the trial by his fiancée, but she had left the court.

Images from the Conlin case. (Author's collection)

Awaiting his fate in Durham Gaol, Conlin proved himself 'an exemplary prisoner', reading books, writing letters, and playing cards and dominoes with his gaolers. Just before 8 a.m. on Friday, 4 January 1929 he was taken from his cell. It was reported that he 'walked firmly to the drop' without comment. As the cathedral clock chimed the hour, executioner Pierrepoint 'drew the lever' and Conlin paid the price for the dreadful crimes he had committed. Afterwards, on the shroud over his corpse lay tulips and lilies of the valley, and a card with the inscription: 'With love to Charles, from Mother and Sister'.

A Bitter Fight for Jobs

South Shields, 1930

Charges:

Sentences:

Inciting to riot
and rioting

Imprisonment
with hard labour
and deportation

South Shields was always more than just a shipping port. As well as serving the needs of industry, it was a holiday resort where working men and their families came from the pit villages, the shipyards and the factories to visit 'the seaside'. It was one of the first towns in England with an ethnic community, where Yemenis and Somalis settled in the 1850s. The Arabs, as they were known, came to work on merchants ships as engine room firemen and stokers, and in South Shields in 1909 the first of the Arab boarding houses opened.

The boarding house keepers recruited Arab men to work on the merchant ships that sailed from the Tyne. The work was plentiful during the First World War, when many of the native seamen sailed on Royal Navy minesweepers, leaving the Arabs to man merchant vessels in an equally important and dangerous role. But the end of the war brought change when returning seamen wanted their jobs back. By then there were about 2,000 Arab seamen in South Shields and there were not enough jobs for everyone. All merchant seamen were members of the National Union of Seamen (NUS) and worked for the same pay, regardless of race. But if the terms of union membership were equal it seems the right to work was not, for indigenous white seamen were clearly of the view that they had priority when it came to obtaining work on ships.

In February 1919 it took Royal Navy sailors with fixed bayonets to quell a riot by the Arabs at the Mill Dam. The issue: the signing up of white men to work on ships. In the 1930s, a new rota system came into force and its aim was to regulate the employment of seamen. The Minority Seamen's Movement, whose leaders were members of the Communist Party, organised a series of peaceful demonstrations outside the Shipping Federation office at Mill Dam, against 'registration'. Registration meant that men could not work on any ship without becoming a member of the NUS and signing a Form PC5, which the Minority Movement regarded as a 'slave ticket'.

On 29 April 1930 there was another riot, this time in North Shields, where the South Shields Arabs routinely went to find work. On that day the steamer *Cape Verde* was taking on crew and an estimated 1,500 white men were gathered on the quay. Thirteen Somalis had been chosen as part of a crew of forty-one, but when two of them failed a medical a scuffle broke out as others tried to fill their places. The Somalis were confronted by a threatening crowd of white men in 'an atmosphere charged with menace'.

An announcement that the *Cape Verde* would not be taking crew that day after all was followed by cheering from the white men and howls of rage from the Somalis. The *Shields Daily Gazette* reported, 'In a firmament of anger [at North Shields] a number of coloured men drawing razors and knives charged the white men, who used their bare-fists as weapons. Police charged, batons drawn, as the outnumbered Somalis fled, pursued by a shrieking mob of mad men and screaming women'. The *Gazette* went on to say, 'The coloured men were dangerous and determined, and it was on these men that the police concentrated ... a coloured seaman with a knife ran up Borough Road and turned to threaten his pursuers; a man with a broom was "badly mauled"; an Arab was struck on the head with a hammer and an attempt made to throw him into the river'. The Arabs were all disarmed, after which they sheltered in the police box to cries from the crowd of 'Lynch them!'

Three Arabs were imprisoned and subsequently deported. A Mr Sydney le Touzel, manager of *The Seaman*, the 'official organ' of the National Union of Seamen, wrote to the *Gazette*, saying that there were four million tons of shipping laid up and 20,000 British seamen idle, and that the Arab boarding house keepers were 'parasites'. Such was the situation in Britain's ports in 1930.

Things came to a head at South Shields on August Bank Holiday weekend in 1930. The weather was sunny, and not far from the Mill Dam picnickers enjoying a well-earned break. The scene was familiar – children playing on the beach, perhaps watching Punch & Judy, and families taking a stroll along the pier. In the austere 1930s, who would have denied them such pleasures? Not the seamen, but then pleasure was far from the minds of those striving to get work on ships.

By then, no Arab or 'coloured' seaman was registered under the rota system at South Shields. That Saturday 2 August, members of the Minority Movement were making rousing speeches at the Mill Dam. One of the movement's members, Peter O'Donnell, told his audience of white and Arab seamen that, 'Pacifist methods have had no result. We have not succeeded in stopping any ships. We will have to use force. We will have to stop that rotten union who are making you sign the PC5'.

Two other Minority Movement members, William Harrison and John Dowell, spoke in similar fashion. Small wonder that by noon, when four

Police responding to calls of 'Riot!'
(Reproduced by kind permission of South Shields Gazette)

The police make arrests. Constable George Errington (left) assisted by another officer and a man wearing a bowler hat arrest two Arabs. (Reproduced by kind permission of South Shields Gazette)

white men were hired to work on the steamer, *Etheralda*, the Arabs were incensed and Ali Hamid called out, 'They work, but there is no work for the black man.' When a party of white seamen happened to pass the federation office to the shipping office, there was 'a rush of Arabs' who carried knives and weighted pieces of wood, and the white seamen were set upon.

The police were ready; drawing their batons, they charged into the fracas only to be met by a hail of stones. Clearly the Arabs were ready too. Four police officers were stabbed: Constables Gash, O'Hare, Addison and Kennedy. They were carried away by their colleagues. The riot moved into nearby Holborn, where dozens of innocent bystanders suffered injuries. All this while families enjoyed their Bank Holiday at the beach, barely a mile away.

On Monday morning, six white men and twenty-one 'coloureds' (as they were described) appeared before the magistrates' court. The results of the weekend's activities were quite visible; seven of the Arabs' heads were swathed in bandages, but seemingly none had received proper medical

In the dock. Arrested Arabs appear before the magistrates. (Reproduced by kind permission of South Shields Gazette)

attention. Ali Hamid was charged with obstructing Inspector Wilson and was fined £3. Fifty-nine-year-old boarding house keeper Ali Saida and four white men, Harrison, O'Donnell, Dowell (an unemployed coal miner) and Dutchman James Smit, were charged with 'inciting to riot'. Two white men, Belgian George Veischelde and William Carnaby, along with nineteen Arabs were charged with 'rioting'.

Fifty-three-year-old Frederick Thompson of London, a Minority Movement 'organiser', was arrested at the Mill Dam on 7 August and charged with obstructing Inspector Scott, who had attempted to move him on when Thompson tried to speak to a crowd when standing on a lemonade box. This may seem insignificant, but there were those of the view that 'professional agitators' were being used to incite trouble, and here was a man who had nothing to do with South Shields. Thompson said he was merely exercising his right of free speech. The magistrates told him not to do it again without first getting permission from the chief constable, or he would 'get into trouble'.

At a further court appearance, charges of wounding police officers were brought against Mohamed Ahmed for stabbing Constable John Adam in the arm; Ali Saleh for cutting Constable Ferdinand Kennedy's finger with a knife; and Ibrahim Ahmed for stabbing Constable Harry Gash. At this hearing the prosecution mentioned the Minority Movement's meetings and the speech by Peter O'Donnell, as well as similar statements by Dowell and Harrison. Harrison had said at the meeting, 'You will have to use force to put the shutters up at the Seamen's Union. The police are always on the side of capitalists. South Shields must be the storm centre. Other ports are looking to us for an example.'

As this inflammatory speech was being made, said the prosecution, Ali Said moved among the Arabs who were now in an 'excited condition'. When, at one o'clock, there was a call for firemen at the shipping office, four white men entered, and Harrison, O'Donnell, Dowel and Smit stood in front of the crowd. Someone shouted, 'Don't let the scabs sign. Stand fast.'

Inspector Wilson said he told Said not to incite the Arabs, and that O'Donnell approached him saying 'there would be trouble' if white men took Arabs' jobs. Wilson saw two policemen struck by weapons wielded by Arabs, and other Arabs throwing bottles and half-bricks. Constable Addison said that when he went to protect white seamen he was surrounded by Arabs, one of whom hit him on the head; PC Addison was stabbed in the shoulder by Mohammed Ahmed. At one point, Dr Harry Crichton was of the view that PC Gash 'might die'. The doctor also examined the Arabs, finding most had suffered scalp wounds, presumably sustained as a result of being struck by police batons.

South Shields Town Hall.
(© Paul Heslop)

The case was heard before Justice Roche at the Durham Assizes in November. Twenty-six prisoners, nineteen of them Arabs, faced charges of rioting, incitement to riot and wounding policemen. C.F. Lowenthal, for the prosecution, said that the boarding house keepers disliked the rota system because, prior to its introduction, they obtained employment for the 'coloured men' who stayed with them, receiving money in return, but Ali Said's influence over the Arab men was entirely destroyed the moment the rota system came into force.

By 2 August no coloured seaman was registered under the rota system. O'Donnell had advised the Arabs that they should use force to prevent men signing on under the new system and had attended the meetings, 'to help the seamen smash the rotten Union of Seamen'. O'Donnell, Dowell and Smit had exhorted the crowd 'not to let any of the scabs sign on'. The Arabs had used sticks and stones, knives and clubs in their efforts to enforce their will.

Unemployed miner Dowell conducted his own defence, saying, 'I do not stand here to defend myself but to indict the shipowner, the National Union of Seamen and the Labour government's police for opening the way for

The statue at Mill Dam, South Shields. 'In memory of the thousands of merchant seamen who sailed from this port and lost their lives in World War II'. (© Paul Heslop)

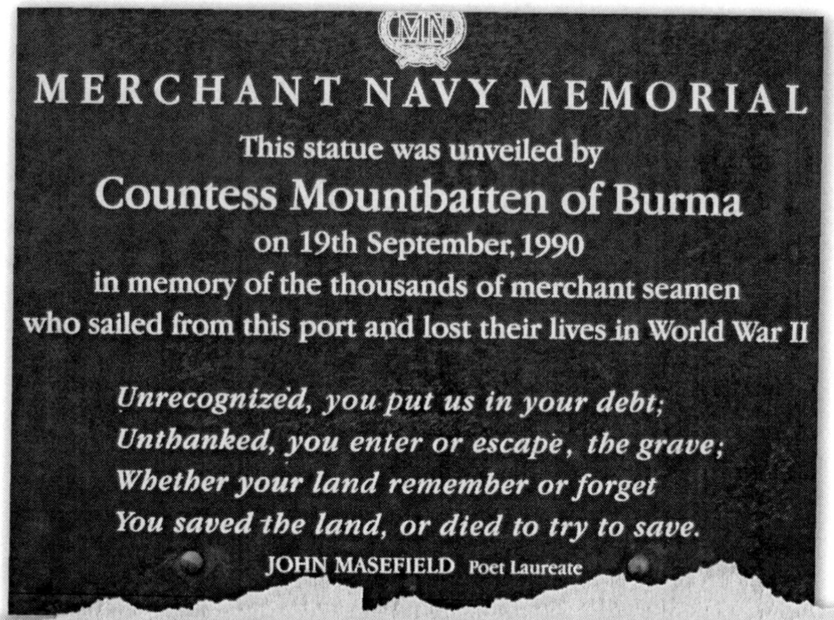

MERCHANT NAVY MEMORIAL

This statue was unveiled by

Countess Mountbatten of Burma

on 19th September, 1990

in memory of the thousands of merchant seamen
who sailed from this port and lost their lives in World War II

Unrecognized, you put us in your debt;
Unthanked, you enter or escape, the grave;
Whether your land remember or forget
You saved the land, or died to try to save.

JOHN MASEFIELD Poet Laureate

The memorial plaque. The inscription makes no mention of the merchant seamen who served in the First World War, including the Arabs of South Shields, who also served at sea in times of danger. (© Paul Heslop)

murderous police officers, incitement to racial riots and the abolition of the freedom of speech. You may succeed in breaking our heads, but one day a new class will arise, not only for better conditions but to take control and power.' He accused a man named Hamilton of producing a steel-lined whip handle and flourishing it in front of the crowd of Arabs, shouting, 'Come on, you black bastards, try and stop me signing on.'

Mr Lowenthal told the jury, 'He is a miner who has never been to sea, talking unmitigated nonsense.'

The judge told Dowell, 'The only question is whether you incited people to use force.' Whatever Dowell's motives, whatever his beliefs about social injustice, his Lordship was right.

Norman Harper, for Ali Said, said there was nothing wrong in intercepting the Arab crew and persuading them not to sign under the new rota system. Hylton Forster, for the white men, said the speeches were 'just the ordinary sort of drivel these people talk'. J. Harvey Robson, for the Arabs, said that they were

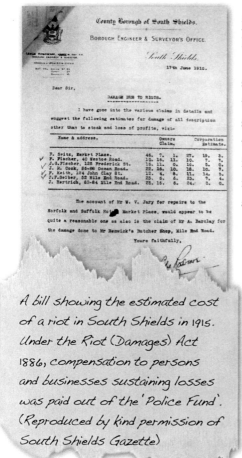

A bill showing the estimated cost of a riot in South Shields in 1915. Under the Riot (Damages) Act 1886, compensation to persons and businesses sustaining losses was paid out of the 'Police Fund'. (Reproduced by kind permission of South Shields Gazette)

just defending themselves against attack. Every man was convicted as charged.

Referring to the Arabs, his Lordship said, 'I think it is very undesirable that men so liable to be influenced should be in this country at a time when there is slackness of trade and it is difficult to get ships. These men in idleness are dangerous here.' All the accused, including the white men, were sentenced to terms of imprisonment with hard labour. He recommended deportation of all of the Arabs, bar two, on completion of their sentences. He also passed comment about the 'undesirability' of Arabs marrying white women, remarking that 'One of them has an English wife.'

Whilst things were 'different' in the past, one recoils at Judge Roche's comments of 'these men', meaning the Arabs being 'in idleness and dangerous'. The men were actually striving for work, not to be idle, and who they were married to should not have required comment from the judge. When Britain was at war and short of seamen, 'these men' served in the boiler rooms of British ships and risked their lives at sea in a time of war – surely they equally had a right to work in a time of peace?

The Arabs should not have turned to rioting and violence, but without being incited to do so by men with a political mission, they may not have. The riots at South Shields were the result of political agitators, many of whom were not seamen, some even travelling from further afield for the cause. Happily, since these unsavoury events took place, the inhabitants of South Shields have lived in harmony and there have been no further riots about race.

The Greedy Widow

Hebburn & Windy Nook, 1955-57

Suspect: Mary Wilson

Age: Unknown

Charge: Murder

Sentence: Life imprisonment

Mary Elizabeth Cassidy was born at Catchgate in 1889, and like many young women she went into service. By the time she was twenty-four she was working for a wealthy builder and she married his son, John Knowles. The couple went to live at Collingwood Street in Hebburn, where they lived for over forty years. They had six children and lost two in their infancy. At some point they took in a lodger, John George Russell, and the three adults lived under one roof. Mary remarked to a neighbour, 'I might as well cook for three as well as two.'

On 31 August 1955, Knowles died after a short illness at the age of seventy-six. Although he had always enjoyed a healthy life his death would hardly have been a surprise, and although prescribed medicine in liquid form for stomach pains and vomiting, he passed away after only a few days. He left Mary nothing. Mary continued to live with Russell but that same year, just before Christmas, Russell also fell ill and he died at the age of sixty-five in January, leaving Mary the sum of £46.

Mary Knowles then became acquainted with Oliver James Leonard, a seventy-five-year-old widower. Leonard knew a Mr and Mrs Connolly who lived at Railway Street in Jarrow, where Leonard would call for meals. He became a friend of the Connollys and when they moved to Albert Road in Jarrow in May 1956, he gave Mrs Connolly £50 to help with the expenses and moved in as a lodger. Soon afterwards Mary Knowles came to the house where, on seeing Leonard, she asked Mrs Connolly, 'Has that old bugger got any money?' she enquired.

'A little, as far as I know,' Mrs Connolly told her, whereupon Mary asked if she could visit 'the poor old soul' in his room. She did so, and afterwards visited the house at least twice more to see him. Eventually, Leonard went to live with Mary at 18 Collingwood Street, Hebburn. Oliver Leonard and Mary were married at Jarrow Register Office on 20 September 1956. After a day or so James Haws, an insurance agent, called to see Mary, who told him she wanted to insure her husband's life, but Haws told her he was too old.

Eleven days later, on 1 October, Oliver Leonard had cause to visit his GP, Dr Laydon, who considered Leonard to be in good health for his age, although with 'signs of chest and cardiac trouble'. He prescribed cough mixture for bronchitis. Soon afterwards, Mary called her neighbour, Mrs Shrivington and said her husband had fallen out of bed. Mrs Shrivington and her sister hastened to the house where they found Leonard lying on the floor; she tried to hand him a cup of tea but he knocked it from her hand. About 6.10 that morning another neighbour, a man called Cunningham, helped to put Leonard back to bed. At 11 a.m., Mary Ellen Russell, another neighbour, called. On arrival Mary asked her to go into the bedroom and see her husband.

Mrs Russell told Mary she thought her husband was dying. 'I think so too', replied Mary, adding, 'I called you because you will be handy for laying him out if he does.' Oliver Leonard died in Mrs Russell's presence – only thirteen days after marrying Mary. Dr Laydon did not see Leonard's body, or even visit the house, but considered his age and his condition and concluded he must have suffered degeneration of the heart muscles and kidneys. He made out a death certificate, recording death through myocardial degeneration and nephritis. Oliver Leonard was buried in Hebburn cemetery and Mary inherited £50.

A few weeks later Mary Leonard had a visitor in George Campbell Leonard, her late husband's son by his first marriage. He had heard about his father's death through his cousin, and George was curious about his father's will. He told Mary, 'I was under the impression I would be a beneficiary, being the only son.' She said his father had left *her* between £45 and £75. When he asked to see the will she told him it was with her solicitor. She said she was the sole beneficiary and that her husband had left him nothing. He lost his temper and accused her of inveigling his father into marriage. When asked how he had come to marry her, she said when he was looking for a housekeeper she took him in and married him at his insistence. 'He couldn't have been in his right mind,' said George.

On 28 October 1957, just over a year later, Mary married seventy-six-year-old Ernest George Laurence Wilson of Rectory Road, Windy Nook in Felling. Wilson was a widower who, since the death of his wife, Clara, had become lonely. He lived a frugal life and disliked cooking so had looked for a housekeeper. Mary would later say that Wilson had advertised 'with a view to marriage', saying that he had '£100 in the Co-op', that he was insured for £50 and had a nice home. Having married Wilson, Mary went home to Hebburn, collected her furniture moved straight into the Windy Nook address.

On 11 November, just a fortnight later, Wilson fell ill and Dr William Wallace attended his bedside. Wilson had been his patient for many years and had not suffered any serious illness previously. Upon examining him, the doctor prescribed

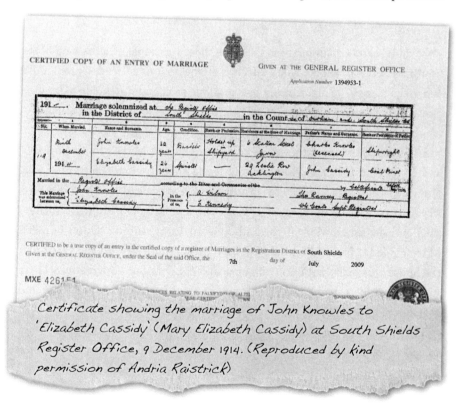

Certificate showing the marriage of John Knowles to 'Elizabeth Cassidy' (Mary Elizabeth Cassidy) at South Shields Register Office, 9 December 1914. (Reproduced by kind permission of Andria Raistrick)

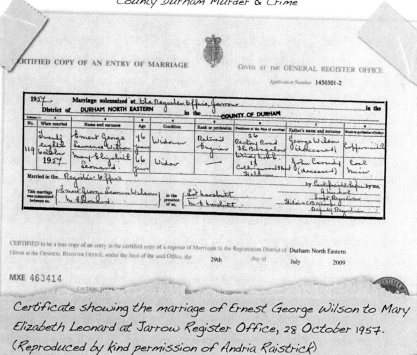

Certificate showing the marriage of Ernest George Wilson to Mary Elizabeth Leonard at Jarrow Register Office, 28 October 1957. (Reproduced by kind permission of Andria Raistrick)

some tablets and cough mixture, believing there was some degeneration of the heart muscle. At 9.30 p.m. Mary knocked on the door of a friend, Grace Liddle, and asked to stay the night, as her husband was so ill and she couldn't stay with him. Mrs Liddle noticed Mary was carrying a shopping bag with a gold watch in it, which she showed her, saying it was her husband's and that she was trying to sell it.

The following morning, the two women went to Mary's house together and Mary told Mrs Liddle she would 'get a shock' when she went inside. She was right. Mrs Liddle saw Ernest Wilson was dead and laid out on a trestle 'with a white thing over his face'. She had to be revived with smelling salts and she asked Mary if she had done anything to him. 'Don't be silly,' Mary replied. Mrs Liddle would later tell the jury at Mary Wilson's trial that the house was dirty, with no wallpaper and cobwebs in the windows. There was a big hole in the bed and the frame was red with rust. Asked if she had ever seen a house as bad, she replied, 'A dog kennel is cleaner.'

That morning, Dr Wallace received an urgent telephone call asking him to call at the house, where he saw that Ernest Wilson was dead. He issued a death certificate, listing cause of death as cardiac muscular failure and myocardial degeneration, which he considered likely to have taken place for a man of his age. The following day Mary contacted the manager of the Co-op, Joseph Milburn, and produced her husband's share book, along with his death certificate, and said she wished to draw out the £100 her late husband had invested. Milburn told her it was not possible and referred her to the probate office. Shortly afterwards Mary drew two small amounts on two insurance policies in her husband's name. Ernest Wilson was buried at Heworth cemetery.

Tongues had started wagging, as Mary had three husbands and a lodger die in little over two years, and sympathy for the recently widowed Mary gave way to suspicion. But if the deaths of the four men had not given the medical men reason to suspect anything amiss, the police, albeit belatedly, also became suspicious, and less than a fortnight after Ernest Wilson's internment they were digging him up, along with the body of Oliver Leonard. Pathologist Dr William Stewart conducted the post-mortem examinations on both bodies and concluded that the men had been poisoned.

On 8 December, the bodies of John Knowles and John Russell were also exhumed and they too were found to have been poisoned. The game was up for Mary who, once the police became involved, left the house in Rectory Road and went to a secret location, known only to police, at the Albert Hotel in Hebburn. At 3.20 p.m. on 11 December she was arrested by Detective Chief Inspector Albert Mitchell and taken to Jarrow police station, where she was charged with the murders of Ernest Wilson, her third husband and the murder of Oliver Leonard, her second.

Mary Elizabeth Wilson stood trial at Leeds Assizes the following March. She pleaded

Wardles', Hebburn-on-Tyne – formerly the Albert Hotel, where Mary Elizabeth Wilson stayed following police enquiries into the deaths of her three husbands and her lodger. (© Paul Heslop)

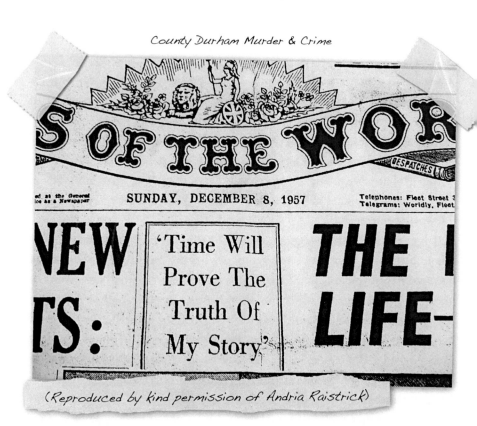

SUNDAY, DECEMBER 8, 1957

'Time Will Prove The Truth Of My Story'

(Reproduced by kind permission of Andria Raistrick)

'not guilty' to the two charges of murder and Justice Hinchcliffe presided. Geoffrey Veale led the case for the prosecution and she was defended by Rose Heilbron. Defence counsel demanded that the two counts be tried separately, but the prosecution argued successfully that the murders proved a 'system', and the jury were entitled to hear the circumstances of both.

Dr Stewart said that Doctors Laydon and Wallace had been wrong in the 'causes of death' on the certificates of Oliver Leonard and Ernest Wilson. In each case, he said, death was due to phosphorus poisoning. Referring to Leonard, he described his heart as 'normal and healthy'; there was no degeneration and no disease. His body had been buried for thirteen months but this did not prevent an accurate examination. He described Ernest Wilson as being 'a healthy elderly man with no serious organic disease'. Death was not due to natural causes, but poisoning. The liver, Dr Stewart explained, is normally chocolate-coloured, but liver tissues are susceptible to poison and change is rapid. Ernest Wilson's liver had 'a yellowish appearance'. Phosphorus, in its elemental form, said Dr Stewart, is not found in the human body and he could think of no way for it to get into the body other than through the mouth.

'*I have nothing to fear*'.
A News of the World exclusive: Mary Wilson 'pens' her story. (Reproduced by kind permission of Andria Raistrick)

Dr Ian Barclay, a forensic scientist, examined the organs from the bodies of the two deceased men and found phosphorus in the stomach, intestines and livers of both. Ms Heilbron, challenging this, suggested it might be unusual to find phosphorus in a body that had been buried for thirteen months. 'It is not unusual,' said Dr Barclay. 'One would never expect to find phosphorus in a liver,' he added. In Ernest Wilson's case tests had shown a positive reaction to the presence of phosphorus. Dr Barclay recovered 2 milligrams of elemental phosphorus from the stomach and 0.7 milligram from the intestines, and both stomach and intestines contained wheat bran. From the examination of this, his opinion was that the phosphorus came from rat or beetle poison, which all contained elemental phosphorus.

The amount recovered from the organs of Ernest Wilson was a fatal dose.

It seems the combined testimonies of Doctors Stewart and Barclay were more conclusive in the case of Ernest Wilson and less so for Oliver Leonard, although Dr Stewart firmly ascribed his death to poisoning. Dr David Price, another Home Office pathologist, said that phosphorus was not found in the human body. He had never seen a case of death from food poisoning which had given rise to livers twice as fatty as Messrs Leonard's and Wilson's. What was his opinion, asked the judge, as to the deaths of the two men? 'They both died of phosphorus poisoning,' said Dr Price.

Mrs Mary Cook said that, from November 1955 until May 1956, she worked in the Jarrow and Hebburn Co-op's chemist shop, which sold Rodine rat poison. She knew Mrs Wilson and had seen her in the street and in the shop, although she couldn't recall whether or not she had sold her Rodine rat or beetle poison.

Ms Heilbron asked Dr Stewart if he had heard of phosphorus being used in pills. 'The French used it at the beginning of the [twentieth] century,' he replied. 'There have been many strange things in pills but I have never come across *elemental* phosphorus.' He was shown a bottle of Damiana pills that had been bought that morning, said Ms Heilbron. After smelling one, Dr Stewart said, 'Yes, there is a little phosphorus in that, at least a smell of it.' Ms Heilbron then read out a list of the pill's uses. 'An amazing assortment,' said Dr Stewart.

Justice Hinchcliffe, the judge at the trial of Mary Elizabeth Wilson. (Author's collection)

Detective Chief Inspector Alexander Mitchell gave evidence of seeing Mrs Wilson at her home at Rectory Road in Windy Nook on 30 November. 'I know what it will be about,' she said. 'I will come with you and help you all I can.' At Jarrow police station, when told it was not thought the deaths were natural but probably due to poison, she said, 'It must have been something they ate when they were out.' The deaths were a mystery to her, she said.

Mary Wilson did not testify. Instead, the defence called William Dixon, formerly a detective sergeant in Newcastle CID, now a private detective. Dixon said that on instruction he had bought a bottle of Damiana pills; the bottle bore the label 'Poison' and no prescription had been necessary for its purchase. He had simply walked into a chemist's shop and bought a bottle of fifty phosphorus tablets. Ms Heilbron maintained that if the deceased men had taken only half a dozen of the tablets phosphorus would be found in their bodies.

Angus McIntosh, also called by the defence, was a manager of a company that made rat poison. He said the bran in his firm's poison was similar to bran used in the manufacture of brown bread or digestive biscuits. The only difference, he said, between the brown bread bran and the bran in his firm's poison was that the bran in the former was more purified. There was no difference between the fragments of bran in rat or beetle poison than that found in brown bread. He had examined a Damiana pill and found it contained elemental phosphorus. How much would each pill contain? 'One-hundredth of a grain, just short of a milligram.' Ms Heilbron said Dr Barclay had found 2.7 milligrams on the body of Ernest Wilson. 'That would be equal to five pills,' McIntosh replied.

'What are Damiana pills used for?' Ms Heilbron asked.

'An aphrodisiac for the treatment of sexual disability and to increase sexual desire,' he replied. Mr Veale asked him if after thirteen months he found that much phosphorus in a body, would it mean that a greater quantity of phosphorus had been ingested in the first place? 'I am not qualified to say,' McIntosh replied.

Defence Counsel, Rose Heilbron, QC. (Author's collection)

Dr Francis Camps, a pathologist, was called by the defence. 'If death occurs in the first phase of phosphorus poisoning,' asked Ms Heilbron, 'what is death usually due to?'

'Heart failure,' Dr Camps replied, adding that the commonest cause of death in a man of seventy-six was a heart condition. Could Rodine be administered as it is? 'A person would have to be blind and without any taste or smell. There is a cloud of vapour as soon as you open the tin. The taste is horrible.' Ms Heilbron asked him whether he was prepared to venture a cause of death in either case. 'In view of the contradictory findings and in the absence of a microscopic examination I would not be prepared to say.'

Mr Veale invited Dr Camps to smell the contents of a bottle, which was

Witnesses for the prosecution: Mrs Connolly (left) and Mrs Russell. (Author's collection)

handed to him. On doing so, he said, 'It smells to me like chlorodyne [cough mixture].'

Veale then stated, 'Both men had a bottle of cough mixture. Would it surprise you to hear there is more than a teaspoonful of Rodine in that bottle?'

'From the smell, yes.'

Veale then said that, 'The cough mixture is an excellent disguise.' The credibility of the defence's witnesses, or lack of it, must have impacted on the jury, for after only an hour and a quarter they returned guilty verdicts on both counts of murder. Justice Hinchcliffe passed the only sentence of death.

There can be little doubt that Mary Wilson murdered Oliver Leonard and Ernest Wilson through administering phosphorus, probably in their cough medicines. As counsel said, cough mixture was 'an excellent disguise', good enough to fool Dr Camps who was unable to detect phosphorus in the bottle that was handed to him (although, let it be said, he didn't taste it). To alleviate detection, the 'foul taste' of phosphorus meant it probably had to be administered in something that had a foul taste of its own; in tea it would probably have been detected. When Oliver Leonard knocked the cup of tea from Mrs Shrivington's hand it was probably no more than a spasm rather than the intended victim being suspicious.

Part of a pre-trial medical report, dated 27 February 1958, during the incarceration of Mary Elizabeth Wilson in the Women's Hospital, Durham Gaol. (Reproduced by kind permission of Andria Raistrick)

Mary Elizabeth Wilson's descendants: Andria Raistrick (left), great-granddaughter by her first husband, John Knowles and her great, great-granddaughter Amelia Lucy Corns. (© Paul Heslop)

A letter written by Mary Wilson to the Home Secretary. (Reproduced by kind permission of Andria Raistrick)

Phosphorus was contained in rat or beetle poison; the attempt by defence counsel to show that it was present in pills fell short of showing sufficient doubt that it was by this means that the four victims had died. Even so, without hearing both cases simultaneously, the jury may have considered the evidence fell short of proof beyond reasonable doubt. But two husbands had died through poisoning, four men in all, over a short period; 'Has that old bugger got any money?' Mary asked of Oliver Leonard. Those words alone showed her intent, along with her interest in money and life insurance policies – she had even intended to sell her husband's watch on the night he died.

Mary Wilson did not hang. Instead, her sentence was commuted to life imprisonment. Even so, after just twelve months, she was writing to the Home Secretary saying her case was 'not proved', and that she was a 'lonely old woman who was feeling her age'. She wrote, 'If you would only gave [sic] me permission to go into the old people's homes I would be most grateful'. Considering that less than three years previously Ruth Ellis, the last woman to hang, had paid the supreme penalty for the murder of just one man, her boyfriend, Mary Wilson, who was convicted of murdering two men, was treated very leniently indeed. She died in prison in 1962, aged around seventy-two.

SOLVED

Bibliography

BOOK

Appleton, Arthur, *Mary Ann Cotton: Her Story and Trial*,
  Michael Joseph Publishers, 1973

NEWSPAPERS AND PERIODICALS

Durham County Herald
Sunderland Herald
Durham County Advertiser
Newcastle Daily Chronicle
The Northern Echo
Newcastle Evening Chronicle
Northern Daily Mail
Shields Daily Gazette
Newcastle Journal

Lightning Source UK Ltd.
Milton Keynes UK
UKOW030751260513